What is it about Eau Claire?

BY BILL SHOGREN

This book was printed in the United States of America.
ISBN: 9781701803008
Copyright © 2019 Bill Shogren

My childhood has never lost its magic,

It has never lost its mystery,

And it has never lost its drama.

All my work in the past

Fifty years, all my subjects,

Have found their inspiration

In my childhood.

Louise Bourgeois

(1911 – 2010)

French American Artist

TABLE OF CONTENTS

ALLEYS

Our Eau Claire, Wisconsin alleys played a big role in knitting our neighborhoods together. "Hello" while hanging wash on the clothes lines, greetings over the fence. Comparing ideas. "How are your tomatoes? How bout the kids?"

Garage doors left open exposed our interests to neighbors. Rev. King (Wesleyan Methodist) had hip boots and wicker creel on a hook and an old dusty calendar showing fishing and hunting scenes — even deer horns hanging on the wall. A small workbench in a corner was strewn with tools. He loved to fiddle with things while possibly pondering his next sermon.

Next to Rev. King's was Erlandson's, and on hot summer Sunday nights, I'd sit in their screened-in front porch listening to yarns about them visiting brook trout haunts in spring cricks and beaver ponds. Sam Erlandson said he heard that some anglers used an angle worm to catch chub, then cut the tail off of it and put the tail on the hook and a brook trout couldn't resist. I had to smile when Sam said his nephews, Ron and Skip, always missed school the day before the opening of deer and trout seasons. Hmmm . . .

I'd stay up till the tree toads and crickets chirped which was my signal to return down the alley to my house. Also, during deer season, Mom would wake me up, and in my pajamas and robe, I'd scamper up the alley to see the white tail deer bucks hinging in their garage. Wow. Was I impressed!

Across the alley was our carpenter neighbor Mr. Elky. His workbench was sturdier and always had boxes of nails on it. It was a place I didn't understand well with its rulers, braces, brackets, wooden slabs, angle irons, and so on. As busy as he was, he always took time to talk.

Often our cars were parked outside the garages. Our dads had their heads under the hoods fixing the thingy, what-cha-ma call it, or thing a-ma-jig. We washed and waxed our cars on gorgeous fall days with the great smells of burning leaves, dried vines, and stems from the garden as we listened to our University of Wisconsin Badgers football games. The dried flowers and vegetable stems had fabulous, rather unique, earthy smells I will never forget and haven't had the pleasure to recapture since.

We had a basketball hoop on our garage and left the ball on the court for any passer-by to take some shots. The ball was never snatched. Our claim to fame was that the future basketball all-star Charlie Mencel shot some buckets on our court. Pretty good chance the BB court was shoveled before our sidewalk.

About every two weeks, we'd hear a tinkle, tinkle in our alley, and when we looked out, it was Mr. Burns with a wagon-full of empty beer bottles covered by a rug. He'd haul them to Shafers' Market to turn in for small change and also get a couple cases of full beer bottles. We never heard the tinkle, tinkle on his return.

We painted our houses and fixed everything ourselves. At least a couple garages had basketball hoops. All of our garages smelled of gas, oil, or soot. Garages were well used.

I slightly remember a truck that stopped in our alley and sent coal down a metal chute to fuel our furnace. On cold nights, Dad would get up in the middle of the night to shovel coal.

We kids played night games in the alley like kick the can and hide and seek. After dark we hocked apples from backyards just out of sight of our houses and played and sang "Starlight, star bright, hope to see the witch tonight". Of course, our alleys were deliciously spooky on Halloween nights.

Brule Carlson, next door, had his Harley Davidson motorcycle in his garage surrounded by tools. He was always tinkering with his Harley. I asked its name, and he said "Mary" after his girlfriend.

We raised chickens, and there was another chicken coop up the alley. Plum and apple trees were popular. There was at least a couple dog houses. We knew most of the dogs' names. I heard that Pearly Brown had a pig named Oscar fenced in next to her garden one summer. Occasionally she even let it loose in her house.

At least once a summer, a clunky old truck came down the alley with a scruffy old man yelling, "Ragman, ragman!" I was told he collected used rags, washed them, folded them, and then resell them to numerous painters, bakeries, and any variety of institutions for their janitors. The ragman also made nice multicolored scatter rugs out of the various colored scraps.

In our big backyard apple tree, Dad and brothers Jon and Bob built a treehouse. I was the biggest user of it. It was there where big plans were made with my friends. From high on the top of the tree, I'd wave to people walking down the alley. Under the tree, we dug a deep trench where we made war plans. I loved it.

Also, under the tree you might see the go-cart brother Jon built for me. We named it Spitfire. One day I walked down the alley to discover three kids standing there spitting on my cart. I said, "Hey what are you doing?" and they said, "Well it's named Spitfire." I responded with "My big brother Jon will be here soon so you better skid-addle." They disappeared between the garage and the shrubs.

In the fall, a neighbor might walk down the alley and witness us butchering our chickens. Dad, with axe in hand, would chop the chickens' heads off on a tree stump. We were totally amazed to see our chickens run around the yard with no heads. They'd stumble and leave bloody splotches in the grass. Then we'd dip the chickens in scalding water to make the feather removal easier. The stench was awful! After we dressed them out, we wrapped them in paper and hauled them off to the commercial frozen food locker across town.

All in all, I have fond memories of our Tin Pan Alley. So easy to remember alley neighbors. Now I have a better appreciation for the positive saying, "Sounds like that's right up my alley."

RAISING CHICKENS

Mother, the "Unsinkable Molly Brown, I ain't down yet." Her resourcefulness saved our dear chickens.

There's always been a little farmer in me, so I was thrilled in 1946 at the age of ten when Mom and Dad decided to raise chickens in our backyard. The idea was kind of a carry over of the recent Victory Garden phenomenon of WWII. Thrifty accountant Dad liked the idea because it was an economical move, and it'd teach us kids some responsibility. I also liked the idea because I never wanted to miss our Sunday chicken dinner after church. We knew zilch about raising chickens, but Mother resolved to see our chicks grow to full size.

We headed off to the Eau Claire Farm Store to buy three dozen chicks. The proprietor clued us in on chicken feed, how to build a chicken coop, and a rundown on the kinds of chicks he had for sale. He explained Pullets (young hens), Leghorns, White Rock, and Barred Rock (black and white stripes). Some chickens were egg layers and some good meat producers. I favored the Barred Rock because they were the prettiest, but practical Mom and Dad decided on the White Rock for dual purposes — good egg layers and great eating. We put the crates of chicks in our car trunk and headed home.

When we arrived at home, we placed our chicks in a marginally well-built fenced pen attached to the backside of the garage adjacent to Dad's garden. Dad had started the coop, but the roof wasn't quite finished. Mother was a little concerned about the unfinished roof, but she understood that Dad was nobody's carpenter, and he sure as heck was too cheap to hire somebody to build us a chicken coop.

We got our chicks in early June when spring storms were a threat to open chicken coops. We kids loved the big storms, and one storm was a doozy. With our swimsuits on, we'd slush and slide on the lawn in the torrents of rain. Just when we were having a lot of fun, during this world record storm, Mom yelled out the door, "What about our chicks?"

I said, "What about them?"

She said, "Willy, they will drown. We need to rescue them." So, I went to the coop to check, and I reported back to mom that I thought they were dead. The chicken coop was totally flooded except for one high spot of ground where all the chicks had huddled, and they looked quite lifeless. Mother was aghast to think we had lost our precious chicks.

Then she said, "Willy, take these big pans and gather them up." I took off my swimsuit, put on my bib overalls and our one old yellow rubber raincoat, my dad's oldest broad brimmed hat, and I charged out there with the pots under my arms and in my hands. In a way I must have been quite a sight in a too big raincoat and man's business hat, sloshing and sliding down to the coop.

It was a mess. The fence was broken open, and the water was about 4 inches deep in most of the pen. I slipped and fell face down in the mud and chicken droppings. Disgusted, I wiped my face with my hands and proceeded to place all the chicks in the pots. They looked ugly and lifeless — just gray globs of thin wet feathers. I brought them to Ma, and she said, "What can we do?"

"Bury them, they look dead to me," was my reply.

All of a sudden Mother said, "By jumpin' jiminy I have an idea. I'll put the chicks in my shallow cake pans and place them in a heated oven for a while."

"Why?" I asked.

She said, "I don't think they're all dead, and maybe we could save a few by drying them out in the low heat of the oven." I rolled my eyes as I looked at my brother Jon leaving the kitchen shaking his head. Mother popped the chicks in the oven. I sat down at the kitchen table; I wasn't going to miss this.

Mom and I sat there for a while occasionally glancing at each other. She seemed so relaxed and sure of herself. I could hardly stand it. This looked like risky business to me. My eyes just followed her as she started to prepare supper. Eventually I could see she had her doubts. But, all of a sudden a "PEEP", then a "cheep" and another "cheep", and then another. We looked at each other, and I jumped up. We went to the stove, and she opened it. She pulled out the rack and there they were-little goldish white puffballs of life. Those little chicks came bopping out of those pans like popcorn popping as they tumbled everywhere. Surely, I was seeing a miracle. They were on the kitchen floor, between the stove and counter, under the kitchen table, and a few tumbled down the basement stairs. What a scene! The two of us with hands, brooms, pots, anything else gathered the fluffy balls. Finally, we got them into deeper pans and put lids on the pans to contain these very revived chicks. Mother and I just sat at the kitchen table and laughed congratulating each other. We lost only one chick. Honest to God, I thought Ma was the smartest person in the world for pulling this off. The next day, Dad didn't hesitate to finish the roof on the coop.

Those were days before garbage disposals. So, besides regular store-bought chicken feed, any food scraps from our plates were fed to the chickens. We scraped our leftovers into an empty coffee can on the kitchen counter next to the sink — everything but the coffee grounds. When the can was full, it was my job to take it out and plop the leftovers into the coop. It amazed me when I returned in ten minutes to find no food on the ground. It was believed that chickens fed that kind of variety produced better meat. I even threw in a few of our very green Granny Smith apples from our backyard tree.

I loved feeding the chickens, gathering their eggs, and talking to them. Over time, I discovered that some chickens have distinct personalities. I named at least three. There was Toughy, because she was kind of mean, pecking at others, Whitey, full feathered and pretty, and then Droopy because she was always last to get in the food line. She also had bare skin showing where others pecked at her.

I took comfort in knowing that our Sunday chicken dinners would continue thanks to Mother's resolve raising our chicks to full size. To me those chicken dinners were a royal feast. Mostly I loved the dark meat with lotsa gravy.

FIFTH GRADE ROMANCE

First dates are a big deal and mine was in the early spring of fifth grade with Geraldine Phillips. Gerri, my first real crush had big dreamy, penetrating eyes, and I did everything I could to impress her. Before the school bell rang each day, I would play kickball in the playground so when I saw her approaching the playground, I would manage to be the guy *"up"* to kick the ball. Once in a while, I would nail a homerun, which was perfect timing to show off in front of Gerri. I even wore a big wave in my hair to look cool for her.

Gerri and I didn't talk much, but around Valentine's Day we passed candy hearts that had words like "You're cute", "Be mine", "I like you", "You're neat", and "Sweetheart". One day in Miss Joflat's fifth grade class, I looked over at Gerri and she gave me a fabulous wink. My heart flat out stopped as I thought, my God, Gerri is a glamorous one. I thought that wink was so daring, so I looked around to see if anybody saw it. We were safe. Her wink thrilled me so much, I winked back at her. This gave me a sweet ache in my chest, and I loved it. We winked at each other that whole year until our eyelids were tired at the end of each day.

Things stayed pretty much the same in our romance till spring when Gerri wanted to go on an actual date. Gerri and I were too shy to discuss a matter of such magnitude, so Gerri enlisted her friend Yvonne Holstein (our go-between) to set it up. Yvonne would approach me in the hallway to tell me the plan or pass me a note. She said Gerri and I were to meet at 1:30 by the swings at our Second Ward grade school playground and walk to the Saturday matinee at the Badger Theater in downtown Eau Claire.

My mother was amused when she picked out my clothes, and I wasn't too happy with a blah brown sweater she chose. It was a beautiful spring day, and Gerri looked so cute with bright ribbons on her pigtails, and she was in a feminine lightweight spring dress. She carried a shiny little black purse and had a sweater draped over her shoulders. It puzzled me what could be in a fifth grader's purse, so I asked. She said, "Oh things." I had a sneaking suspicion the purse was empty, and she carried it to complete her outfit thinking a date was such an important affair she needed the special effect. It appeared that she had prepared better than I had because she looked perfect, and my heart filled with good feelings toward her. Sensing that this real date was important to her, I knew I had to do my best. Pride welled up in me because we were the first fifth graders to go on an actual date.

Gerri and I walked the mile to the show. I was a little tense and impressed with how much more relaxed she appeared than I did. She didn't talk much, so I tried to think of things to say. "What did you do this morning?" I asked. She said she baked cookies with her mom. I told her my favorite cookies were chocolate chip, and she said the cookies they made were plain, which I took as sugar cookies. "What about your favorite song," and she said, "Ole Buttermilk Skies". I told her my favorite was "Buttons and Bows" that I heard on the radio sung by, according to my mom, Dinah Shore.

She said she knew I was the catcher on the baseball team and that my hero was Yogi Berra, the great catcher for the New York Yankees. I told her I liked Yogi better than the Brooklyn Dodgers all-star catcher Roy Campanella and that I was trying to get Yogi's baseball card and I even try to walk like Yogi. I'd seen him in the sports newsreels before recent movies, so I knew he walked with short, quick steps. She looked at me with a sly smile when I told her that some of us guys on the team chewed Switzers licorice so we look like we're chewing tobacco like the big league players. We liked to spit the brownish juice on the ground. "The guys on my team are starting to call me Yogi, because I'm the catcher. So I guess that will be my nickname," I said proudly, while wistfully looking back at Boyd Park seeing my buddies playing baseball.

9

We arrived at the theater a couple minutes late, and I remembered that my brother told me I'd have to pay for everything on a date. Luckily the movie was a Hopalong Cassidy cowboy show, which made it easier for me to fork out the moola. After I paid 12 cents for each show ticket, I bought both of us a box of popcorn and a Milky Way bar. That was twenty cents for popcorn and ten cents for candy bars and 24 cents for the movie. A grand total of 54 cents, which shot this and next week's allowances, a ton of money to me. I was broke. It kind of bothered me how fast money went on a date.

We walked down the aisle during the previews looking so attentively at the screen that when we sat down, I made a mistake. With my left hand I lowered the seat two seats from Gerri's. When I sat down it hit me. Geez I'm not sitting next to my date, how dumb. It was so embarrassing, I worried that Gerri thought I was too shy to sit next to her, and she might wonder if her date was a dud. Feeling if I got up and moved next to her to that empty seat I would feel self-conscious in front of the crowd, I was paralyzed. So, like a dope I sat through the whole show with an empty seat between us.

After the show we walked home discussing the movie. She agreed that Hopalong was neat in his black clothes and hat with white handled pistol, and she loved Topper his pure white horse. Actually, I was more relaxed, and we had a better conversation than when we walked to the theater. Gerri seemed more like a girlfriend. Encouraged, I went on about how I had seen enough Gene Autry and Roy Rogers movies and besides Hopalong I liked Lash LaRue movies because Lash's weapon was a bullwhip. With his bullwhip, he'd wrap the whip around a bad guy and yank him out of the saddle. He could also eject a pistol out of a guy's hand or holster with his precision whipping. Gerri seemed moderately impressed.

About a week later I heard from Yvonne Holstein that Gerri wanted a second date. Actually, I was just happy how things were going with the winking. This dating stuff seemed a bit much. In my heart I was content knowing that I was Gerri's boyfriend, but I wondered what Gerri was thinking. My head started filling with thoughts about what was expected of me. Would I be expected to hold her hand? I had heard about how the older guys put their arms around girls in movies. My brother told me how that worked. You just put your arm up on the back of her seat and then very gradually drop your arm softly on her shoulders. Brother Bob said that was more ninth or tenth grade stuff. In my heart I knew I was ssoooooo not ready to try any hand holding and such. It was in the last days of school, so I made up excuses for no second date by fibbing that I had a baseball game. Gerri and Yvonne stepped up the pace by trying to fit in date times. The "wheels were turning too fast" for me, so I kind of let time run out and summer break arrived just in time. I knew that I was a chicken and that I wasn't ready for the responsibilities of a real romance.

During the summer our paths never crossed and alas our romance dwindled to nothing. It was sort of easy for me to fill the days with baseball, fishing, mowing lawns, and helping my brother on his very large paper route. I thought about Gerri over the summer and thought we might rekindle our flame in sixth grade. Two days into sixth grade and not one wink told the story. My fear was that if I winked at her she might not wink back and that would be hard to take. I was afraid of the truth.

Fifty years later, Gerri and I met at a class reunion and embraced each other. We talked a little about our fifth-grade romance, and we concluded that we had something special. We didn't discuss the winking and the empty seat between us at the theater. We laughed when we hardly remember anything about the movie.

GRADE SCHOOL ROMANCE AND BEYOND
Sixth Grade

In sixth grade, romance takes new turns with stronger emotions. To us boys, it was important to win the favor of the cutest girl in class. All of us guys were simply nuts about Deanna, the ever-popular blond, blue-eyed American beauty with the cutest smile. We knew she'd be hard to get, but we had to try. She was nice and friendly, and I felt I had a small advantage because we were in the same Sunday school class.

Tommy Benson was the lucky one who sat next to her sharing materials such as glue, paper, and scissors during art period.

Our problem was how to be around Deanna outside of class. Recess and noon hours were our only opportunity. During those breaks we always devised plenty of playground games. Even in winter we had outside games to play. Lucky for us, the woodlands of central Wisconsin had light, fluffy snowfalls. After our playground got its first base snow, all new snows were perfect for playing tackle pom-pom pull away.

The special gift was that Deanna was one of two girls that would play with us boys. The other girl was Goopy Riley. Our game, pom-pom pull away, was played by having one person in the center of the playground and a big group of kids on one end of the playground. The person in the center would yell "pom-pom pull away," and the big group would try to get across the playground without being tackled. As kids were tackled, they would go to the center and help in the tackling of the rest of the runners that tried to cross the course each time. Finally, there would be one fast running, quick dodging person still standing who was the winner. That winner would be the next single person to take the center and yell "pom-pom pull away" to start a new game.

My big plan when the games started was to be the first one in the center so I could tackle Deanna and roll in the snow with her. This dreamboat might be impressed with my speed and tackling ability. I would zero in on Deanna and rap my arms around her legs, hips, or waist and take her down. Once when we went down, my face rubbed up against her rosy cheek. That cheek was so smooth and soft, I daydreamed about that magic moment in arithmetic class that day. Needless to say, when I was one of the runners, I would do my very best to not get tackled so I could get in the center again and get another shot at Deanna.

The neatest thing about making physical contact with Deanna was that when we'd collide, she would let out a loud "ugh", which made it seem so personal and gave me a certain rush. I don't even think the other guys caught unto my scheme. Maybe it was also kind of a competitive thing in me knowing that I was acing out the other admirers.

I discovered that there were additional reasons why tackling a girl like Deanna was much more fun than tackling a boy. Her strength impressed me. She was just as strong as a boy and struggled as much. Another nice feature was that she smelled nice. There was a certain pleasant scent on her coat. It was news to me that girls that age wore real perfume. Later my mother explained that maybe she used a shampoo that smelled good and that scent transferred from her hair to her coat collar. Eventually I discovered that almost all girls' coats had a nice scent to them. I liked that.

After about four games that winter, I did feel a little guilt about taking liberties with Deanna with hugs under the guise of an innocent playground game. I worried that she would catch on, but she never showed it.

After recess or noontime, our class would return to our room with snowy pants. The snow in my cuffs and seat of my pants and socks would melt and cause discomfort, but it was worth it to me.

Eventually reality set in, and we boys had to face the fact that none of us were anything special to Deanna. In time, all us guys found girls that were more equal to us in looks that we could call girlfriend. These girls made us feel like actual boyfriends — there was a comfort in that fact. Shamelessly we had a list of girlfriends. Seemed like we all had a list of about two or three girlfriends in order of how we adored them. My list was: 1. Patsy 2. Marilyn 3. Lois. Of course, in our fantasy Deanna was number one.

Sixth grade passed, and the next fall we were in the big junior high school with hundreds of kids from grade schools all over town. Everything sort of went back to square one. All of us guys found new girls to have a crush on. After school and on weekends we started taking the bus, our bikes, or walked across town to see our girlfriends.

ANNA'S "RENASCENCE" MOMENT

While reading poems by Edna St. Vincent Millay I was struck by her "Renascence," which reminded me of my grade school classmate Anna Bluedorn and how she tried to jump high enough to touch-feel the sky. This passage grabbed me.

>So here upon my back I'll lie
>And look my fill into the sky.
>And so I looked, and, after all,
>The sky was not so very tall.
>The sky, I said, must somewhere stop,
>And sure enough! I see the top!
>The sky, I thought, was not so grand;
>I 'most could touch it with my hand!
>And reaching up my hand to try,
>I screamed to feel it touch the sky.

Pedaling like mad on my all decked out red and white Schwinn bike, I came to (with the help of just enough sand on the street) a dramatic, sliding at a glance, stop, to talk with Anna in front of Bluedorn's Greenhouse. We didn't really know each other all that well, but she seemed approachable, so we had a friendly greeting, which resulted in a curious conversation.

15

Anna said, "Boy, look at those clouds in the sky. I wonder if I can jump high enough to touch a cloud?" I nearly dropped my bike as I thought how curious. Anna went on, "Maybe if I huff and puff and give it all I've got, I can feel a cloud."

She looked inspired and it seemed like she wanted to make a big impression on me, even with this goofy idea. She bent her bony knees, and with big blue eyes, huge wide smile, blond pig tails bouncing, she jumped with great oomph and got about one foot of air. She looked at me, still all lit up and said, "Whew, I guess I'm not jumping very high today, but I sure would like to feel a cloud."

I took that as her not giving up the notion. Shaking my head, I patronized Anna by congratulating her for a really great effort as I jumped back on my bike and headed home.

Some people with great imagination see things differently from ordinary folk. The great poet William Blake as a small child told his parents he saw God's face staring at him through his bedroom window. At age nine Blake claims to have seen a tree filled with angels, and in his late teens William claimed he walked out to the edge of the heath and reached up and felt the sky. This last one may have been a pipe dream. So, Anna was in good company with her heightened imaginations.

CHASING BASEBALLS

Seems as a kid, in the 1940's, I only got a bright spankin' new white baseball on my birthday. Early in the season Eau Claire parks department furnished a big green wood box at Boyd Park with a few baseballs but it didn't take long for them to disappear into thin air. Some of us had one or two scruffy balls — some sort of water-logged.

To garner better baseballs, we'd go to our nationally registered baseball stadium at Carson Park. This grand stadium was built in 1936 by the WPA (Works Progress Administration) for the Eau Claire Bears out of sandstone quarried near Downsville, Wisconsin. Some of us were members of the Knothole Gang who sat beyond the right field. From there, we gravitated to the stadium and got down behind the Bears dugout. The players were warming up before, "Let's play ball."

Our mission was to mooch balls from the players warming up sort of between the dugout and the bull pen. We'd say to them, "Hey, how 'bout giving us one of your old practice balls?" We knew their practice balls were really in good shape. Maybe two out of the five requests we got players to toss one over their shoulder to us. We thanked them profusely.

Another way to get balls was to stand outside the stadium and watch for pop-ups over the stadium and bleachers. The balls would usually land among the trees and grass. There would be a big scramble of about eight guys rushing as fast as possible to grab the ball. It wasn't always the fastest kid who got the ball, but often the toughest in the pile-up. I must say, for all the scuffles, I never saw an actual fight break out.

One summer the Eau Claire Bears team got a skinny kid out of Mobile, Alabama named Hank Aaron. Hmm, we saw how he panned out.

Another thing we did to equip ourselves for softball was to be a batboy for a church or tavern league team. Seems like every game there was a batter who cracked a bat. The two batboys would scramble to be first to grab the bat. We took the bat home and pounded a nail in it to help close the gap, and then very tightly wrapped black tape to finish it off. We thought it was nice to have a backup bat, but to be honest we never used them so they wound up in the garbage can or insinuator.

But come spring the ice rink covering our baseball field would start to melt, turning grey, then puddled, turning it dark brown, then light brown. We could then take to the field, Joe DiMaggio, Babe Ruth and Yogi Berra tagging our new baseball into the outfield all the way to where the sand-burrs started.

BIG DAY AT FERN GROVE DAIRY

Finally, in 1947 at the age of nine, I was going to leave kid stuff behind and work like a man on my uncle's dairy farm in north central Wisconsin. For my birthday, I got a pair of Oshkosh B'gosh bib overalls, and I was anxious to use them. It just seemed to me any place that produced food made the world go around. Farm kids worked every day, not like us city kids who traded baseball cards, played ball, checkers, read comic books, and fished our river that rendered mostly rough fish. The farm is where I could pretend being older because on the farm a kid is expected to do big work.

Mother brought me to the bus depot for my first long-distance bus ride, and I proudly carried an actual suitcase with some clothes in it. It surprised me when the Greyhound bus driver grabbed my suitcase and stored it in a big compartment underneath the bus.

Off we go in this huge, silent, smooth bus. Of course, I figured the bus would drive directly to my cousins' town, but the bus stopped, it seemed to me, in every small town between Eau Claire and Cornell. All these stops drove me nuts. Come on! I imagined myself saying to the bus driver. I got so desperate I even thought of doing the grownup thing of reading the book Fur Trappers of the Old West Mom handed me when we said goodbye. But

19

I was too excited to read, so I just gazed out the windows at the farms, lakes, and small towns along the way. When we reached Cornell, I was surprised that the bus depot was the pool hall.

It seemed to me my cousins' dairy farm was a big deal because on the side of the big yellow barn, looking smart and stylish, were the words Fern Grove Dairy in white letters with green trim and a green fern for a flourish below the name.

That first late afternoon, cousin Jim showed me their heifers in the barn. It was hard to believe how the heifers would first suck on my fingers then eventually my entire hand to get salt from my skin. The heifers made a slobbery mess on my hand, but I didn't care. I just wiped it off on my pants. Jim called cows *bossy*.

It thrilled me to be around big buildings, equipment, animals, and smells. Everything was bigger. Even the sweeping storms from the broad open skies, the wide-open pasture and meadowlands made the rain seem closer, stronger, and more threatening.

In the woods next to the farm, I saw a deer for the first time and heard some grouse drumming on a log. My cousins said every once in a while they hear a wolf howl late at night in their woods.

The Henrickson's had two beautiful red McCormick Farmall tractors. After seeing these beauties, I felt that Farmall's "red line" must be the standard for serious farming. Aunt Grace had promised me I would learn to drive a tractor as well as the team of horses. How big is that!? Already I was thinking about how I'd tell my friends back home about these big jobs.

Cousin Charles showed me the part of the barn where they stored huge blocks of ice in sawdust. The sawdust insulated the ice blocks so well they didn't melt in the summer heat. This flabbergasted me. The ice was used to cool the bottles of milk during the milk route delivery. Everywhere I turned was something new and interesting to see. I even witnessed cows chewing their cud. Of course, the farm had a chicken coop, pigsty, and a tractor building with dirt floor that smelled of grease. There was the building where they pasteurized the milk which had a pleasant smell of milk and stainless steel. Next to that, the tool shed had big weird looking tools such as sledgehammers, axes, chains, ropes, assorted buckets, horse harnesses, and thick leather reins hung from the walls.

Hard to believe it, but there it was. . . the bull on a heavy chain. The bull was brownish black and huge. Everybody told me to steer clear of the bull. Bulls are dangerous because they're always ornery. And, "Whatever you do never wear red. Red infuriates them."

I said to the bull, "So you're the bull that gored Uncle Chick's brother Allen." I was impressed, but when nobody was looking, I slowly crept up to the bull to see how close I could get while leaving myself a quick retreat route. All of a sudden, I noticed that his chain had more length than the distance between him and me. At that moment, the bull's eyes met mine, and my heart stopped as I slowly inched my way backwards while softly telling the bull, "Now bully bull, don't get excited. I'm leaving you alone. I'm not here to bother you, only to get a better look at you." We parted company on good terms.

Back at the farmhouse that night, Aunt Grace admonished, "We go to bed early on the farm. I'll wake you bright and early at 5:00. Because the hired hand was sick, I would help deliver milk and the haying operation."

Sure enough, she woke me with, "Milk is delivered early, you know." I figured Aunt Grace would make me one of those famous farmer style breakfasts of ham and eggs, but instead she served homemade white bread toasted, and Cheerios.

After breakfast with the sun peeking over the trees, Uncle Chick and I filled the milk truck with white and chocolate milk and plenty of ice. Chocolate milk was my favorite, and because I was helping the boss, I figured I could drink all the chocolate milk I wanted. Alas, I wasn't in control and got no free drinks.

The beautiful lettering, **Fern Grove Dairy,** on the side of the truck and on the milk bottles impressed me. It made me proud to be part of running an honest to goodness business.

Chick knew everybody on his milk route by their first names. He said, "The housewives never even bother to look good when it is only me at the door. They treat me like family, I've known them so long."

21

Even though the milk truck was less than a year old, the driver's seat already had stuffing and springs sticking out. Chick explained that hauling steel milk crates in and out of the truck and making frequent stops caused wear and tear in just a few months.

The pace was slow, and it seemed like Uncle Chick could do the route in his sleep. All of a sudden, I got my first lesson about economy. Bringing an empty bottle to the truck from a front porch, I spilled some change from it into some tall grass. We searched but couldn't find the money. Uncle Chick admonished that I be more efficient and said, "You lost important money." From that point on I was the model milkman's helper.

After delivering our last stop at Fern Groves biggest customer, Camp Nawakwa, we headed back to the farm. I had worked hard and learned an important lesson about handling money, and I felt I grew a little from the experience.

We arrived back at the farmhouse at 1:00, and the table was set for midday chicken dinner. I was starving. I loved the dark meat with lotsa gravy. The table on the back porch had a red and white, checkered tablecloth and tons of food. On the farm the noon or midday meal is called dinner, and the evening meal is supper. There is nothing quite like a whiff of fresh baked bread cooling on the porch railing to make me swoon. Aunt Grace told me that all the food came from their very own farm. Hard to imagine, but I believed.

It was haying time! The men from the neighboring farms came rolling in on tractors pulling hay wagons. They all sat down for the feast, talking a mile a minute and eating like mad. Most wore laced up leather boots, straw hats, and bib overalls. Chick told me it's traditional for surrounding farms to help their neighbors in the big events like haying and thrashing. Hay has several uses on a farm, and it had to be cut at just the right time. I was expected to do a man's job today. I figured I was up to the task.

After dinner we headed for the fields. To me this would be real farming — toting bales of hay and riding on tractors and hay wagons. What could be bigger to a city kid? The crew boss let me drive the tractor for one length of the field. The feeling of sitting so high up on a steel seat with holes in it seemed weird but rather important because this was the first time I had ever driven anything. Mostly my job was picking up bales in the field and throwing them unto the hay wagon. I took off my shirt because I wanted that farm boy tan.

Those bales of hay started to get pretty heavy, and about every fifth bale had a garter snake under it, which startled me. Getting bushed early, I dosed off between some bales of hay. Moments later I was discovered by the crew boss who with a big smile said, "Is this too tough for a city slicker?" I'm thinking, what the heck, I'm just a kid. Another lesson learned. The sun was high in the sky, the temperature in the 80's, and the work was never ending.

I needed a break, but I knew I had to be a worker so sheepishly I asked the boss if I could be the guy to run back to the farmhouse to fill the water jugs for the gang. He smiled and said, "Sure, all the jobs are equally important, and we work as a team." Which made me feel good.

Finally haying ended, and I saw a trail of tractors and hay wagons winding down the gravel road returning to neighboring farms. In my simple mind I thought it neat how the Lutherans and Catholics got along come combining time. What an afternoon. I was dog-tired and very sun burned. Aunt Grace applied salve to my nose, back, and shoulders.

Back in the house I thought I'd found a haven. But, all of a sudden Uncle Chick announced, "It's milking time." I thought gad, I trust he doesn't want me to milk cows. But of course, he did. So off we go. Uncle Chick explained to me that they blend the milk from the Holstein for their high volume and Guernsey for their high fat and protein to get a better quality Fern Grove milk. To my relief I noticed a few automatic milking machines being used. Chick of course required me to milk by hand which rather surprised me. I struggled at first but eventually got the hang of it, and I managed to milk enough cows to make me feel like I contributed something. Wait until Mom, Dad, brothers Jon and Bob hear about this. It was that night Aunt Grace told me how to talk about farming. "Don't just call us farmers. It connotes dirt and hard labor. Ask them if they farm, which connotes ownership of a business."

The next day the bus to take me home left at 2:00 PM. That morning I was treated to a ride in the open back of the pickup truck, and Allen, Chick's

23

brother and business partner, explained that the open back was designed to haul things that are always needed in the daily operation of a farm.

Allen hitched up a two-horse team to a large wooden wagon, and I drove them out to the pasture so we could check on a cow that was calving in a patch of high grass. Sitting high up on the horse drawn wagon, holding those reins, and having such large animals go exactly where I wanted them to go made me feel like a boss man. I more closely felt the sheer power of the animals, and unlike the tractor, I felt connected to the horses. That fascinated me; we were a team of three. I couldn't believe how often these huge horses swished their big tails. Later Allen explained that this team was trained through so much repetition that the person holding the reins really doesn't have to do a thing. That didn't matter to me; I thought they were responding to the strict commands of my voice and handling of the leather reins. I couldn't wait to tell my baseball team back home at Boyd Park.

It was then that Allen laughed and said, "Too bad your dad isn't here because every time he's here he leaves with cardboard boxes full of cow pies for his garden." Allen explained that Dad selected just the right cow pies. Not too soft and not too hard (dry). We both got a laugh when Allen quoted Dad as saying, "If I ever have an accident, how will I explain to a highway patrol guy about cow pies strewn on the road?"

All in all, I was simply dumbfounded with all the work farming required. Lessons were learned all right as I worked so hard in these two days. When I was delivered to the bus station, Charles told me that his dream was to come to my big city. He was so serious about how he yearned for just playing cards on shaded screened porches, going to a swimming beach, and seeing movie after movie after movie.

Now that I am grown up, I reflect on all I learned on my cousins' farm. The farm family lived right on the cutting edge of life. Every single day the whole family faced the economic realities of the commodity and livestock markets. This was never discussed at my supper table. The farm people repair all their own buildings and machinery. Such valuable knowledge to grow up with. When I was a kid, I romanticized about that life. My cousin Charles wanted what I had. He couldn't get to my much bigger town soon enough.

BIG RED

My third-grade teacher in 1945 was Miss Helen Adler, a hulk of a woman with red hair and freckles. Quite strict, a no-nonsense teacher of the first degree.

One day I was messing around with Gretchen Schultz, who sat behind me and Adler came to me, grabbed my arm and yanked me up. She proceeded to say, "Listen here, William, don't bother my best student! Your foolishness is not welcome in my classroom." I thought I'd faint. Adler went on with, "You'll stay after class as long as I feel like keeping you."

And so I stayed after class looking at the clock on the wall wondering where she disappeared to for so long. Time was ticking by and it was 4:45PM I thought Mother must be wondering where I was because we usually ate supper around 5:30. Forlornly looking out the classroom window I could see the ground was too wet for baseball but with the spring runoff it was perfect for playing in the fast gushing gutters with our little gray plastic battle ships we got from the dime store. The two sloping blocks on Summer Street between Emery and Main St. were perfect to watch our ships float and crash into icy edges and other ships.

Another game I could have been playing with my buddies was marbles. I owned only six marbles and one steel shooter, which was larger than our marbles and called a "steely." Marbles season usually lasted about one week. We had to find dirt, which wasn't abundant because there was still some snow on the ground. Often, we'd find the alley was best to draw a circle on the ground with a stick and drop our marbles in the center. With our heavy steely we'd knock the other guy's marbles out of the circle. We really didn't play the game like it was supposed to be played but we had fun anyway.

Bored as could be, I gazed out the window of this third story room and spotted Adler crossing the street and heading either for her car or to catch the bus. I thought she forgot me, and if I didn't open the window to yell at her she'd catch holy hell from Principal Stokes and my parents for leaving me stranded. I had to think fast, relishing the idea of getting her in trouble. But I decided to holler at her, "Hey what about me?" She stopped across the street looked up at me, and yelled back, "Oh, my God, I forgot about you. I'll be right there."

When she opened the door, she was so apologetic and nice. She said she was visiting with another teacher in that teachers' room and then just left for home. I was set free.

Trundling home I thought about what I'd tell Ma. OK, so I was held in detention, which to me was no big deal. It happens. But the bigger crime was how Adler messed up by keeping me too long. I'd deflect the blame off me and onto her.

Well that didn't fly. Mom earnestly suggested that I had no business getting into trouble in the first place and that Miss Helen Adler had a reputation as a good teacher, albeit strict, and she was a personal friend of Mom's from their days at Eau Claire Wisconsin State Teachers College.

BUNDLING UP

Oh yes, on the coldest days Mother would say, "By the jumpin' jiminy I'll get you all bundled up." Even though we lived only a block and a half from our Second Ward grade school she'd see to it we wore long underwear, two pair of gloves or mittens, at least two sweaters and a coat, plus galoshes over our shoes. She'd throw in a scarf for good measure. I remember when I was a little twerp, Mother bundled me up so much, she could have just given me a shove out the door and I would have rolled to school.

I never paid much attention to the weather. The word blizzard wasn't in our vocabulary. The snows in our north central Wisconsin forest lands were light and fluffy, coming straight down.

On the coldest days and nights, I skated at Boyd Park. Sure, we often went just once around the rink and then headed for the potbellied stove in the warming house. But skate we did, even when there were only half dozen skaters.

Even in bitter cold, we sledded at seven bumps hill next to Forest Hill Cemetery. I'm surprised we didn't get hurt more often. There were long and short sleds. The sleds had names like *something* Glider, Slider, or Flyer. The little sleds were light in weight, faster, and really gave us a thrill when we hit a bump (always our goal), and our sled being so light and small, we rarely landed on it.

The Eau Claire Country Club Golf Course offered good opportunity for downhill skiing. There was one hill so steep, it was named suicide hill. I fell my first two tries, but on my second day of trying I made it all the way without a spill. I had arrived. The Forest Hill ski scaffold in my neighborhood was torn down, so we were practically the only part of Eau Claire without an official ski jump. But the several slopes on the golf course were good enough for us to build our own ski jumps out of snow.

Whoa, the weatherman is talking about a sub-zero cold snap heading our way, so I'd better *bundle up*.

CAMPS

There was no talk of summer camps in our house, but I should have gone to camp. I loved everything about it. In my youth, there were YMCA and YWCA camps as well as private girls' and boys' camps, church camps, Boy and Girl Scout camps, and I suppose, just plain camps opened to all. The biggest camp I knew of was Phillips Boy Scout Camp near Rice Lake, Wisconsin. This huge camp was given to the scouts by the industrial, philanthropic Phillips family of Eau Claire.

Both of my Boy Scouting cousins attended Camp Phillips camp every year. I envied them terribly. Because both of my brothers didn't go to camp, I was denied the opportunity. "We treat all three of you boys equally" said dad. I thought, for goodness sakes Jon and Bob don't even have an interest. So why deny me?

A great memory for me was visiting Camp Nawakwa with my Uncle Chick. The camp was originally a boy scout and later a girl scout camp. Chick was my dairy farming uncle who pasteurized his own milk and delivered the milk daily in Cornell and the surrounding areas. On this day, I was his helper. Nawakwa was the last stop on the milk route. Everybody loved my uncle. Especially the camp director. This was still a girls' camp, but the director cut me loose to wander around the camp on my own. Down near the dock, I could see huge bass swimming by. I got so excited, the director told me the next time I helped my uncle on the route, I should bring my casting rod, and she'd allow me to make a few casts for those bass. No doubt Chick was the influence behind my invitation.

Another nice memory for me was when I visited my Mother's oldest living friend in Eau Claire. Helen Stewart was the very last vestige in Eau Claire of my parents' friends. I wanted to know what reminiscing with her would be like. I called her by phone, and she said, "Come on over, Billy." Her apartment was very nicely appointed, and she told me she was ninety-eight years old, and her doctor said she'd live to be one hundred.

We were having a nice long conversation, when suddenly she stood up and explained she had something to show me. She opened a drawer and pulled out a photo of a girls' camp she attended in days of yore. While showing it to me, she explained that the dwelling they slept in was open aired except for a canvas that dropped down on each side of the beds at sleep time. She said the hoards of mosquitoes were horrendous. Never had I ever imagined such a Spartan camp. Helen related that with so much swimming, kickball, bonfires with hotdogs and roasted marshmallows, vespers at night, and handicrafts, they'd drift off for a good night's sleep after swatting mosquitoes for twenty minutes.

What a curious thing talking with Helen. I felt like I was getting in on something special. When I got home, I sent her a long, handwritten letter. The next year, I called only to find out she had moved to a care home. When I called there, Helen told me she wasn't up to seeing me, and the following year, I called and was informed she had passed on. The care home said she made it to one hundred years old. I smiled and said to myself, "By golly, you did it, Helen. Good for you, and thanks for the charming last chat when you shared the camp photo with me." To this day, I get a lump in my throat when I think of dear Helen Stewart and how she expressed her love of summer camp. Was it because it was her first time away from home, the special camaraderie of being with girls only, catching a sunfish off the end of the dock, or the first time she discovered the wonders of nature? Who knows what memories will stay with us forever? In the end, what photo will we pull out of the drawer?

CHRISTMAS WEEK AT BOYD PARK

My love for Boyd Park is deeply rooted in me because in summer it was our baseball field, in fall football, and in winter our ice skating rink. On the rink, we'd see people of all ages practicing racing, figure skating, playing games like pom-pom-pull away, crack the whip, and couples skating arm in arm.

No matter where I am in the world, the nice smell of the night air and the wood burning takes me back to that wonderful warming house and the pot-bellied stove. The aroma permeated the whole neighborhood. The house was an old wood shack attended by a retired city worker, we called Old John. There was abundant heat, and it seemed to me that Old John was over dressed with his wool cap and pants, wool checkered black and white lumberjack shirt, suspenders, and lace up leather boots. He never spoke much and did his job. Outside was a pile of oak logs. Coming or going, the door slammed loudly. Old John was a tobacco chewer, and he knew he couldn't spit outside the house because brown splotches wouldn't look good and we couldn't count on fresh snow to cover the spit. So, John would slowly walk over to the stove and with a black steel poker unlatch the silver door handle, open the door, and spit on the red, hot logs. We'd hear the sizzle.

From the ice to the warming house was a walkway of wood slats. There was a bench in the house that wrapped all the way around the walls for skaters to use while slipping their skates and galoshes on and off. Surrounding the classic black stove was a railing where we dried wet mittens and socks. The trick was to get them close enough to the heat for a quick dry without burning. Sometimes a wool mitt got charred, and the pungent smell was awful.

A curious thing about skating at Boyd Park was I never remember it being too cold to skate. I only remember going skating every night, except when the rink was flooded that day. When it was bitter cold, we'd swing around the rink once and come in to warm up. Ol' John kept pouring out the heat.

Going to and from the rink on really cold nights some kids complained that their toes got too cold. Not mine. My slick system was having only my galoshes over my wool socks so there was space between my feet and galoshes. This didn't allow the sub-zero temps close enough to freeze my toes.

Christmas Eve day was always a big skating day for me. I simply was beside myself waiting for Christmas Eve to arrive when we'd open our presents. To make the time fly by, I'd spend the entire day at Boyd Park. I would look at the sky in late afternoon for the first hint of darkness. The warming house floodlight was turned on at 4:30 which was a good sign.

On the Christmas Eve day of my fourth-grade year I took a different route home by crossing through our grade school playground. The school building looked so lonely but venerable in the encroaching darkness. The cold was different than on the rink. It was a stark, calm shroud that encapsulated me. Hardly making it out in the darkness, I was thrilled to see the classroom windows with our Christmas season artwork pasted to the windows for all to see. There was my jolly Santa, Ellie Gilbertson's star of Bethlehem, assorted angels, and Tommy Benson's goofy Christmas tree that looked more like a decorated green oak tree. I stood in four inches of fresh snow and thought what a waste. This is the exact kind of snow cover we wished for our tackle pom-pom-pull away. And none of us here to take advantage of it, but another week and we'd be back at it.

I knew that when I got home the front porch light would be on, Aunt Mae from Chicago would be there, the Christmas tree would be glorious, and we'd get our presents after supper and after the dishes were washed. As I stood there, it dawned on me for the first time in my life that Christmas is the greatest.

The day after Christmas Day, the rink was the busiest and most colorful winter wonderland like a Grandma Moses painting. There were girls with brand spanking new white figure skates, colorful scarves, caps, mittens, and socks. The long wool scarves were a favorite of mine because they had showy bright colors and because of their length bounced around the skater. A few people donned new jackets, and some girls wore tight black ski pants. I loved the girls in their jackets with fur-lined hoods. White jackets to me seemed elegant.

During Christmas week of my sixth-grade we boys learned some social graces at the rink. Yes, of course romance was in the air. Any young boy can tell you the girls look especially cute with cold rosy cheeks and noses. A couple of us guys would say to these girls, "Would you like me to help you with your skates?" The girls looked so fabulous when they'd say, "Oh sure." The girls sat on the bench, slipped their skates on and spiked the back end of the blade on a log in front of them. We boys would press a finger where the skate laces crossed when the girl pulled the laces, or they would press their finger, and we'd pull the laces. We felt like young gentlemen and of course we figured we were winning the favors of the popular girls in our class. For me after the skates were nice and snug, I'd sneak a little caress of their ankles with my hands. There was nothing like soft white leather skates around a sweet ankle.

Another social grace we learned in sixth grade was how to skate with a girl. I mean, really skate with a girl! We'd go up to some junior or high school girl and ask, "Can I skate with you?" The girls were always willing. We would put our right arm around her waist and our left hand held her left hand, as we skated. Usually we floated once around the big rink. I liked it best when the girls wore simple knit wool gloves or mitts. That way I could feel their hand better than if they wore puffy mittens. There was a certain sensation, like a current going between us, which made it seem like I was really feeling her, more personal.

There's a warm spot in my heart for those older girls who made us young boys feel so good by skating with us. One girl I skated with was perfect. She was very pretty. She wore tight black ski pants and a waist length white parka with a fur-lined hood. At the end of our whirl around the rink she did a perfect figure eight, then the most exquisite bow with her arms gracefully unfolding in front of her. I thought I would melt. To me, this dreamboat seemed like a performer from Shipstads and Johnson Ice Follies on her day off. These gals would say nice things like, "Thanks, it was nice skating with you sir," in kind of an ironic way. Or they might smile and compliment us on our skating skills. At any rate, they lifted our confidence. I had one girl say, "I don't understand why you boys don't give the girls your own age a break, twirling them across the ice," as she gave me knowing wink.

The thought of skating with girls our grade left me breathless. Maybe she'd turn me down or while swirling around the rink I couldn't think of what to talk about-a diversion I needed to take the attention off the fact that we were holding hands and my arm was around her waist. Finally, I worked up the nerve to ask Maxine Brandt, a good skater and a real sweetie, to swirl around the rink with me. We did it in good form.

Someone said that when one tastes a good wine, they're lucky enough to pick up the taste or scent in that wine that takes them back to a fond memory. I've had that fortunate experience of smelling, even tasting in a glass of wine, the wood burning in that warming house stove at my dear Boyd Park so many decades ago.

CIVICS LESSON

Baseball was in the air. You could almost hear the bong a block away when our baseball hit Ellie Schmidt's head. On those gray blustery spring days, we boys would watch daily for any sign that our Boyd Park skating rink, covering our baseball field was rotting and turning gray. We knew once the ice went, our baseball field would be exposed, and we'd be back out there batting, running, catching, and pegging the ball.

Weeks before this we boys got our baseball mitts oiled up. We went to our basements to get the brass oilcans. This was before aerosol cans. I guess Dad bought oil from the gas station or hardware store and opened the can of oil with a sharp pointed opener and poured the oil into the long-necked brass oilcan. I loved that long neck oilcan with its thick, rich sounding ger-gunk, ger-gunk, ger-gunk when I pressed on the bottom. We kneaded the oil into the palm of the gloves, placed an old baseball in the center, and bound up the glove tightly with twine. Then the glove sat until we started playing catch. This could be one day or a week away. By then a nice soft pocket had formed in the mitt ready for the ball to settle in. This was a neat thing to do because we heard that the Eau Claire Bears professional players used oil to break in their gloves at the beginning of each baseball season.

Now we were set; just needed the baseball diamond to dry out which seemed to take forever. In the meantime, we started playing catch in the playground at school.

One day during recess, Tommy Benson, Rollie Jacobs, and I were really winging the baseball in a three-way catch when Ellie Schmidt walked right into our line of fire. Ellie went screaming into the school, and the playground monitor came up to us and said, "Boys, it is time to put your baseball and mitts away." We three looked at each other dejectedly.

Rollie said to Tommy and me, "Isn't that just like Ellie. She's such a drip. I think she is a little nutty."

I had a queasy feeling the rest of the day, thinking we might be called into Principal Stokes' office after school. Sure enough, we got the word from our teacher that we were to meet with Mr. Stokes and the playground monitor.

Our principal wasn't a very engaging type; he never spoke to me in the halls and seldom changed the expression on his face. He was dark complexioned, short, swarthy, had bushy eyebrows, and wore thick glasses. I thought he dressed a little too casual with his solid colored shirts and knit neckties that were squared off at the end. His trousers didn't match his corduroy sport coats. His shoes might have been Hush Puppies. I thought him so different from my accountant dad who wore gabardine suits, bright striped ties, white starched dress shirts, and businesslike wing tip shoes. To me Stokes didn't look authoritative. For all I know, he may have been ahead of his time in 1950 in his casual wear.

It didn't take us long to find out that this casual looking grade school principal could indeed be business like. He started out in a low stern voice, "I understand you rambunctious boys hurt one of our students while playing catch during recess," and he looked straight into our eyes.

I said, "Ellie walked right into the ball. It wasn't our fault."

Stokes looked at the monitor, then scowled at me and said, "You don't say. Well you have a lot to learn, William." Right then I felt that familiar sick feeling in my stomach as I remembered that Mr. Stokes and my mother attended Eau Claire State Teachers College together. I thought, cripes my mother will find out, and I'll catch holy hell.

Then Principal Stokes looked at Rollie and Tommy and asked, "What do you have to say for yourselves?"

Rollie said, "Everybody knows she's kind of odd and anyway she was in our territory on the playground. We thought the girls were supposed to stay out by the sidewalks and skip rope and play jacks. The main playground area is for us boys, isn't it Mr. Stokes?"

With his bushy eyebrows and his thick glasses, Stokes glared at Rollie and said, "Who do you suppose the swings in the middle of the playground are for? Boys only? We lowered the basketball hoops from ten feet to eight feet to encourage the younger kids to use them. No boys, you are wrong if you think that older boys have free rein on the playground. The entire playground is for every child, boy or girl, kindergarten through sixth grade. These are not rules made up by me. The rules apply to all the schools and are set by the Eau Claire School Board. I must say that I agree with these rules wholeheartedly. It is the only fair way. I have noticed that some boys, (not necessarily you three), seem to think the center of the playground is for boys only, and they are sadly mistaken."

Tommy looked scared stiff, Rollie had kind of a smart aleck look about him, and I just pretended to look interested in what Stokes had to say. Stokes went on, "Boys, I know you are good kids. You are doing well in class according to your teacher, and I hope you learn from this incident because as you travel through life, you will have to learn to be fair and believe in equality, so you might as well get used to it. I hope you know the meaning of the word equality. It means equal for everyone. I have no choice but to prohibit any playing catch with kitten balls (softballs) and baseballs on the playground. It is the only safe way. Let this be a lesson to you, a lesson in civics. You will hear a lot about civics as you grow older, so learn to share and play fair now so you will avoid conflicts in the future."

Mr. Stokes went on to say, "There is nothing wrong with Ellie Schmidt. She's a nice girl with a lot of imagination. And that imagination will serve her well someday. Tomorrow before class with our playground monitor present, I want each one of you boys to apologize to Ann."

We agreed and were dismissed after he mentioned that none of our parents would be notified about this unfortunate incident as long as we apologized to Ellie. I don't know about Rollie and Tommy, but I was relieved that my mom and dad would not hear about this meeting. Not that I thought this was such a big deal, after all it was an accident, but I wanted a clean slate. I knew that eventually they would find out about something more serious I did wrong, and the less I had on my record the better.

To my mind we got through the apology to Ellie in fair shape. The playground monitor did look a little askance at us boys because we were slightly wimpish, and we didn't look into Ann's eyes. I think our tone of voice seemed rather insincere. Ellie loved it though as she beamed with delight, pleased with the attention.

We three boys walked home together that day and started out grumbling about the injustice of it all. Tommy said, "I think girls are a real pain. I should know, I have two sisters."

I said, "By the way, Tom, why didn't you talk in Stokes' office?" Rollie and I did all the talking."

Tommy just shrugged his shoulders. We all walked and talked and eventually agreed that probably the whole playground is for all students, and we shouldn't hog the biggest part, and Mr. Stokes was right. Rollie piped up, "It isn't Stokes' deal anyway. It's that school board or whoever makes all the rules." By the time we got to our homes it seemed like we were all trying to impress one another by being understanding about sharing the whole playground with the girls and the younger kids.

Nothing changed much on the playground after that. Only that we suffered from not playing catch. We were still waiting for the ice to thaw. Ellie never seemed to hold it against us for beaning. She seemed to really like boys, and she was her old self, goofing off with us in the halls. During recess and lunchtime Ellie usually spent her time playing jacks on the sidewalk. The girls never came into *our* part of the playground, but we ventured into their spot on the sidewalk where they jumped rope and played jacks because Tommy had a crush on Marilyn Meyers, and I was winking at Gerry Phillips.

One thing we boys did learn was to jump rope. I messed up the first two tries as I got tangled in the rope. After that I figured it was all timing, so I stood back to watch the long rope being twirled by a girl on each end, and I figured the best time to scoot in was about a second before the rope slapped on the sidewalk. Getting the timing right got me in with the girls as I jumped rope like crazy.

I liked the way the girls chanted a song in cadence with the slapping of the rope on the sidewalk. We guys jumped rope for about two days then sort of drifted back to the basketball court to shoot baskets during recess and lunch break. Lois Jordan was the only girl that came our way, and she was always included in shooting buckets.

Finally came the big day. The baseball diamond dried out overnight, and we fifth graders were back out there tagging that ball over the fence again. In our dreams!

DOING BUSINESS

Finally, at the age of nine it was time to start my first serious business. Enough of shoveling snow and mowing lawns for money. My friends and I dabbled with Kool Aid stands in front of our houses that barely made any money. So, Dad suggested I set up a stand down by the footbridge that lead to the big Gillette Tire factory. Half of the workers crossed the bridge to get to and from their jobs. That struck me as a great idea. We both thought it best to be there when the workers let out at 4:00 PM. Surely, they'd be thirsty for such a luscious drink.

With Mother's help, I loaded my wagon with two flavors, grape and cherry — plus some Dixie cups and a small wooden match box with some coins for making change. With high hopes I very carefully pulled my wagon the long two and half blocks to the footbridge.

The whistle blew and I readied myself for the rush of workers. They came in shifts, it seemed. They looked like they could use a refreshment, but the first group passed me by. One guy said that a bunch of the factory workers stay an extra half hour to shower which was arranged by their union and Gillette paid them an extra fifty cents for that. News to me.

Worker after worker walked by, ignoring my pitch. "Ice cold Kool Aid, Grape or cherry." After an hour it dawned on me that this venture wasn't worth it, so I trundled home with a measly two dimes for my effort. I could hardly believe it.

Undaunted, a week later I decided I'd try my luck selling the apples from our backyard apple tree. I'm not sure what kind of apples we had but they were big and green all summer. In late August and September, they ripened and turned yellow. Possibly Granny Smith apples.

Again, with Mother's help, I packed the apples in brown bags of three different sizes and priced them 10, 15 and 25 cents. The next day I loaded my wagon and set out. I started my route on Main St. and headed north. I rang the doorbell at every house and gave my pitch, "Would you like some apples that make great apple pies?" I got more rejections than takers, but the product was much pricier which made it OK.

This was a little harder work with lugging the wagon and walking up sidewalks and steps. To be honest I think some of the buyers just bought to be nice with no apple pie in mind.

After Main St. I crossed over to Emery St. and headed toward home. I hit a few more houses and made a couple more sales. By then I was rather tuckered out. There was just enough room in my wagon for me to lay down. So, I thought maybe I could take a nap in front of Duane Evenson's house.

I really couldn't sleep but I closed my eyes for a while. Then all of a sudden, I felt a bump on my wagon, and I looked up to see two guys on bikes. One said, "What the heck are you doing?" I told them I was selling apples for pies and they laughed and said, "Who'd ever buy green apples?" My response was, "Not many, I must admit." With that they rode off and I headed for home.

All in all, the venture was sort of too tough for the little jingle in my pocket, but it was more than my weekly allowance. It totaled seventy-three cents and I must have counted it four times that day. In a small way felt "*I was on my way.*"

Truth be told, my earnings usually went to firecrackers and sparklers on the fourth of July and most anything on the midway of the Chippewa County Fair, especially cotton candy and freak shows.

My childhood business experience was fun but arduous. Lessons were learned and it taught me how to plunge into business enterprises.

DOING THE COOKING

Honestly, I can say I've never been intimidated by what goes on in a kitchen. I started out in 1948, my fifth-grade year, by helping Mother with Norwegian Christmas baking. Mom moved a stool to the kitchen table so we could work in partnership. Then she put a way too large dish towel on me for my apron. With sleeves rolled up to my elbows, I was ready. Baby, did we bake! With her strong guidance.

There was Julekake (Christmas bread) with cherries, raisins, and pieces of citron. Rosettes, which I loved because we dipped an intricately designed iron full of wet dough into boiling hot oil to get it crusty. Then we sprinkled them with powdered sugar. Of course, another favorite was Sandbakkles or what some folks called sand cake-great smelling dough pressed into tart-like metal shells and then baked. It was a little tricky getting the dough in the shells just right, so Mother admonished that I be sure to press it evenly and smooth the edges perfectly. She said, "Remember Willy, our Christmas baking has to be great looking too, because Christmas is a happy time of year. Friends will stop by, so we'll serve them our goodies looking festive." Then we started a batch of Norwegian spice cookies.

I asked Ma where the heck she got all those recipes, and she answered, "Oh, different friends like Hanna, Ruth Berg, Marion Bennett, and Julia Erlandson. Good Eau Claire Scandinavians, ya know!"

When I was in sixth grade, Mother started teaching across town at Robbins School. Dad was an accountant at Northern States Power Company downtown, a mile or so from our house. He loved to walk to and from the office and never carried a brown lunch bag. Apparently, he didn't care to eat downtown, so it was decided because he had an hour for lunch, he would walk home. I'd scurry home from school to be there with a meal already cooked for him and me. We'd get a good hot meal, and Dad liked the economy of it. It was a big responsibility, but I managed it.

This was a time when Hormel had canned hamburgers and wieners, Spam, and corn beef hash, just to name a few. I cooked canned creamed style corn, Dinty Moore beef stew, and plenty of Campbell's soups. I served Spam and Tweet sandwiches. I liked the twisty key thing for opening cans. Often for dessert, I'd served our own canned fruits. Sometimes at our noon meals we wouldn't eat all the canned corn and fruit, so I would seal the containers with the soft plastic covers that had the stretchy strap feature to make a snug seal. Into the Kelvinator refrigerator they went.

If time permitted after lunch, Dad would sit and read his *Philatelic* magazine, reread yesterday's *Eau Claire Daily Telegram Newspaper*, or peruse *The Lutheran Home Companion* periodical.

Thinking back, I feel it wasn't the mechanics of cooking that impressed me. After all, it was simple cooking, but the fact that Mother had the confidence in me to handle the responsibility made me proud. About all my older brothers, Jon and Bob, did in our kitchen was make peanut butter sandwiches and pour a glass of milk. I thought, how many kids my age cook like I do? I never screwed up one meal. Since then, I've never winced at trying new cooking techniques with a variety of foods.

ESTELLA SCHOOL

As a grade schooler in the 1940's, I finally got to visit my cousins' one-room country school. Cousins Charles and Jim lived on a dairy farm about two miles from school. They'd tell me stories about their school having one row of desks for each grade. There were four rows with one teacher, and they had to use an outdoor toilet. Geez, I could hardly believe it.

In 1947, Ma and I travelled from Eau Claire to Cornell during my Easter break. For some reason, their Easter break didn't coincide with my school. Mom and I stayed overnight at my cousins' farmhouse so I'd be ready to jump on the bus for a ride to Estella School. A school bus? Holy smokes, I'd never been in one, and I was itching to go.

After breakfast, we packed lunches and walked down Hendrickson's lane to the gravel country road to wait for the bus. It rained like crazy the night before, so it was hard to find a place to stand and wait. But finally, I spotted the yellowish/orange bus. It was all muddy on its bottom and had crusted tires.

We jumped on the school bus. What a clatter of laughter and shouting! They all looked and asked about me. The bus was so interesting with its roaring motor and driver in overalls and plaid flannel shirt changing gears with the floor stick shift.

We arrived at school, and right away I spotted the bell tower. I said to Charles, "I didn't know your school had a big bell and the building was all wood."

When getting settled in the schoolhouse, I smiled about the setup of one row for each grade. We had to locate an extra chair for me at the end of Charles's row. Right away the teacher announced that they had a visitor from the big city of Eau Claire, and everybody stared at me.

The class started with arithmetic. Our teacher asked one girl for the answer to an adding problem, and she had the answer. But another little harder adding question was asked of another kid and he didn't have the answer, so the teacher turned to me and said, "Well, we have someone from the big city, and I'm sure he'll know the answer." I felt a little anxious, but luckily had the answer. The teacher smiled with satisfaction. This inquiry happened a second time with subtracting numbers, and I answered correctly. The teacher seemed pleased, but I felt self-conscious thinking she put me above her students. This made me feel uncomfortable. Firstly, because I thought my cousins and probably other kids were smarter than I was, I didn't want the other kids to think just because I was a big city guy I was smarter than they were.

During recess, cousin Charles, his two buddies, and I were walking around the small playground in front of the school when some rascal following us kept stepping on my heels. After the third time, I got miffed and decided to use my right leg to swing back and catch his foot as it was stretched forward to make me stumble. Sure enough, I caught his foot, and he fell backwards into a big puddle and got his whole right side soaked in mud.

We returned to the school room, and to be honest, I felt good about being lucky enough to have the answers in arithmetic, but I also showed how tough I was.

FAST BREAK

How can I ever forget how dazzled I was with my first trophy? I won it playing for my Second Ward grade school basketball team when we got all the way to the city wide fifth grade championship. We (the Eastside Hill gang) went up against the Ninth Ward (the North Side gang). The trophy was a team trophy, not a trophy for each individual player. We were so proud.

Our team included Bob Barneson at center because he was the tallest, then the next tallest Bryn Carlson and Leroy Anderson were the forwards, and Tommy Benson and I were the guards because Tommy and I were the shortest and the quickest. We didn't think anything about not having substitutes. The other team had one sub.

The tournament was held at our Eau Claire YMCA. My oldest brother Jon decided important games like this required a coach, so he took on that task for our team. During warm up it was obvious that the Ninth Ward was as good as we feared. They had Jack (Lefty) Rada at guard and Virgil Nelson handling center. Lefty was the best athlete our age in Eau Claire. We knew him from football and baseball, and I knew he was an ace speed skater. Lefty was a stocky bulldog with quick, nifty shifty moves, and he could really sink buckets. Virgil was big and tough, and we all knew it would be hard for Barneson to guard him.

Because Lefty was swishing so many in the warmup, Jon thought we'd better come up with a secret weapon. He gathered us up and said, "I'm going to show you guys how to run the "Fast Break." We had heard about the Fast Break but had never used it. Jon explained that, "When the other team shoots at our basket, Bill and Tommy should run like a bat out of hell to the other end of the court, and Barneson should get the rebound and just wing the ball down court to us guards so we can take the ball in for an easy layup." Jon emphasized that we shouldn't even wait to see if Bob got the rebound, but just run immediately so as to really get the jump on the other team.

The first minute of the game Barneson got the first rebound and winged the ball down court so fast and far, the ball bounced out of bounds untouched.

Jon yelled, "Where are our guards?" Benson and I obviously were a little slow on the uptake. We guards quickly made the adjustment and made sure we did our part from that point on. We racked up quite a few points with the Fast Break that first half.

Our team led all the way to the end of the third quarter when the Nine Ward team caught on to our Fast Break. Their guards started to play better defense against our Fast Break and pretty much took that weapon away from us. Lefty was so good at weaving in between defenders that he got a lot of lay-ups. He also started gunning buckets like crazy out around the free throw line. Lefty had his best game, and we lost by four points.

The Ninth Warders got a nice champions trophy, so we thought maybe our school would only get a ribbon or medal. Low and behold, when Tommy and I went up to the director of the tourney to receive our teams second place award, it turned out to be an actual trophy-a full six inches of gold metal on a two-inch base. We were dazzled. This was a time when trophies were really something. We were impressed with the weight of our award. The gold-coated metal was solid, and the base was stone. It was not like today's lightweight trophies with their cheap hollow metal and plastic bases with everybody on the team getting a trophy. Even though we got second place, we all thought Jon was a great coach with his Fast Break. I kept thinking about how proud we'd be on Monday when our school would see the trophy in the glass case on the first floor. I must admit that my thoughts were more about how my heartthrob Geraldine Phillips would be impressed with me. To my disappointment Geraldine showed little interest in our basketball accomplishments.

The teams showered in the YMCA locker room. Benson and I brought the trophy in to show Anderson and the guys. We all were giddy with pride, and then Bryn Carlson touched the trophy with his wet finger, and somebody said, "You can't touch a trophy with a wet hand because it will leave a mark on it forever." But, no big deal, we were so proud.

Sixty some years later while in Eau Claire I stopped by the Second Ward grade school to see the trophy. Sure enough, there it was in the trophy case. I went into the school office to inquire if I could handle the trophy. An assistant principal got out her key, opened the case, and handed me the trophy. By gosh, the spot Bryn Carlson left on the trophy nearly sixty-five years ago was still there. I asked the assistant principal, "If when you move to the new school, would all these things in the case go along or would our trophy end up in a box in a school district warehouse?"

She said, "Oohhh nnoooo, it surely will be displayed in the new school. That's part of our school history."

The first words out of Bob Barneson's mouth at our fiftieth high school class reunion were, "Where is Jon now? What did he do with his life? He was a good coach."

GIVING BACK

I'll never forget my seventh-grade basketball team at the Eau Claire YMCA. Our team was mostly east siders, but luckily, we recruited Lefty Rada, the north-sider. Lefty was the best player of our age in town.

To play in our Y league (called the Bush League), each team needed colored shirts, so we would look official. My team's color was red, and most of our parents went to Longs Sporting Goods store and bought nice red basketball jerseys with numbers sewn on the back. At least one of our teammates couldn't afford to do that, so his mother used red dye on his strapped undershirt. With pieces of fabric like flannel, his mother cut out and sewed numbers and the team name on the dyed shirt. Nobody thought much about it.

Our team names showed little originality as most teams chose existing local mascots. There were the Stars of course, then the Old Abes. Old Abe was a bald eagle mascot during the Civil War and the Eau Claire High School's mascot, chosen because a lot of us had a hero on the ECHS team. Then the Shamrocks same as St. Patrick's Catholic High School, made up mostly of boy's attending Sacred Heart Junior High School. Their shirts were green with white numbers. My team was the Pro's, and finally the Badgers, like the Univ. of Wisconsin — a little hero-worship again.

Our tennis shoes were black canvas high top with white rubber soles, toes, ankle patches and smart looking white laces. There were two makes of tennies — Converse and PF Keds. Keds were the cheapest, so that is what our team wore. The richer Third Ward team wore mostly Converse. On the Converse tennies' white ankle patch, in red letters it said, "Chuck Taylor All Star". We thought that was so neat. Taylor was an All American basketball player out of Manhattan College or New York Community College in days of yore. Our socks were all wool sweat socks. A couple of our guys begged, borrowed, or took without asking their older brothers padded leather knee pads so they would look like hot shots. So, there we were, a rag-tag looking team with shorts that didn't match and red shirts with one lighter that the others. This was the first time in our lives we wore an actual basketball shirt with a number and team name. In our minds, we looked like a solid team, and we played our guts out.

We junior high school guys were in awe of the senior high school players who practiced shooting in the gym from time to time. In particular we, loved watching Charlie Mencel with his classic jump shot. He was always swishing them. Charlie practically lived at the Y. With the help of Clayton (Andy) Anderson, the Y's youth athletic director, Charlie learned to play the game better than anybody in town. Anderson saw the innate talent and desire in Charlie and nurtured that in him.

Mencel eventually went on to be a high school All American at Eau Claire High School, college All American for the University of Minnesota, Big Ten MVP, and he advanced to the professional ranks playing with the Minneapolis Lakers Pro team.

It was when I met Jim Theormar of Eau Claire at the Minneapolis Oakdale tennis courts that I learned that Charlie Mencel and his friend John Schaaf started the Clayton Anderson Memorial Golf Tournament fund-raiser, out of a debt of gratitude for what Clayton Anderson and the Y did for them during their youth.

Andy was the YMCA sports activities director during the 1940's, 50's and 60's. He was very devoted and exhibited special mentoring skills. Being in charge of the youth basketball program, Andy showed us how to have more fun with sports while building character. There are thousands of men all over the country that realize how Anderson and the Y made a positive impact in their lives.

To me, Andy Anderson was the ideal grown up model, and I wanted to be like him. He looked like an athlete because he had a nice physique, and he was the first person I knew who wore sportswear. I had never seen warm up pants or a monogrammed sweatshirt on anybody. In stunning red and black lettering on his sweatshirt, over his heart, was YMCA, and below that, in smart looking bright red, was ANDY. He looked so sporty to me.

In my mind, Andy had a perfect job because it was all sports. Sports was all I cared about. I wanted to be an athlete. Anderson was a hand's on type of instructor. He treated everybody equally, and no matter how poorly I demonstrated an athletic skill, he would praise my zest and admonish me in his gentle way. I always remember leaving the Y feeling lifted by Andy. Even back then I knew we were lucky to have him at our Y.

All the way through grade and junior high school, I went to the Y every Saturday morning during winter and early spring. Besides learning the rules of the game, Andy taught us how to shoot a layup, long shot, free throw, and how to pass and guard, as well as the rules of good sportsmanship. All the while, Andy, through example, demonstrated the core values of the YMCA: "Caring, Honesty, Respect and Responsibility."

Besides helping thousands of local resident boys, the Eau Claire YMCA provided a good service for the community when it came through for the future major league world record home run hitter, Hank Aaron. Aaron arrived in Eau Claire in 1952 to play for the Eau Claire Bears baseball team. The Bears were a minor league farm club for the Milwaukee Braves. Hank Aaron might have struggled to find a private residence or a commercial lodging establishment to take him for the whole summer. The YMCA was there with open arms, and Hank got a permanent room. When Hank moved up in baseball to become the V.P. of the Atlanta Braves baseball team, he had a policy of not paying more than $100.00 a night for a hotel room. One day in a hotel lobby in Los Angeles with his ex-teammate and friend, Frank Benevides, Hank turned to Frank and said, "You know Frank, it may be silly sentimentalism but I feel that the best room for my money was back during that lonely summer in 1952 at the YMCA in Eau Claire. Every day

I got two fresh fluffy warm towels. I loved that. It made me feel like a king, and I got the room for $5.00 a week."

Every year in August, approximately 400 men from all over the country return to Eau Claire to golf, play tennis and socialize at the Clayton Anderson Memorial Golf Tournament. This wonderful fund-raiser is designed to raise money to expand youth sports programs at the Y. Charlie Mencel, John Schaaf, and other participants donate $1,000.00 each year. The event through donations, auctions, fees, and concessions raises over $35,000.00.

When I saw Charlie Mencel at the tournament a number of years ago, I said, "Charlie, I'd walk into the Y basketball courts at 9:00, and you'd be shooting buckets. I'd come back at 11:00, and you'd still be shooting, then at 1:00 and again at 3:00, and you'd still be draining them." Charlie's head went back as he laughed, and he said, "That's it. We'd go to the Y on Saturday morning and stay all day, except when we went across the street to Woolworth's dime store for a bar-b-que hamburger and glass of root beer."

It makes me happy to attend this golf event and reconnect with this group of men to share inspiring stories and the feeling of appreciation for what we got out of the YMCA experience. Some of the older guys laugh at what a value the $6.00 yearly fee was, while my age group does the same remembering our fee of $9.00. Try as the Y did to keep the annual fee down, the fee got to $21.00 a year by the late 50's. A couple guys commented that the Y wanted the yearly fee in one lump sum, but that was tough for some, so Andy pulled strings and got the payments stretched out over two or three installments.

We also laughed about the guys who would pop into the Y just to get a shower. Some of the kids from large families had one bathtub in the house. So, a shower at the Y was a welcome relief once or twice a week.

Clearly, we kids learned some good lessons back then, and the lessons have endured all these years. We learned about fair play, teamwork, and never quitting. As I socialized with the participants, I appreciated that the Young Men's Christian Association's mission statement was being lived out every day through these men: **We build strong kids, strong families and strong communities.**

the flying eagles and the school yard jump

FLYING EAGLES EAU CLAIRE WIS

BY RON BUCKLI

GOOFY SKI JUMPS

It must look crazy to southerners seeing people on skis coming down a steep snow-covered scaffold and lifting off the end soaring 100 to 400 feet through the air and landing on snow. Where I grew up during the 1940's in Eau Claire, ski jumping was a tradition. Wherever the Norwegian immigrants settled in the north, they built ski jumps, and our town once had seven. Kids started at about age six, and the Fourth Ward Grade School had a scaffold and landing knoll in the playground. The kids jumped before school, during recess, at noontime and after school. Eau Claire ultimately produced some world-class ski jumpers such as Billy Olson who participated in the 1952 Winter Olympic Games in Oslo, Norway and in 1956 in Cortina, Italy.

By the time I came along, The Hilltopper's scaffold above Forest Hill Cemetery near my house was getting too rickety, so was torn down and never replaced. I always felt sorry that the old jump was gone because I knew it was a huge advantage to have a jump to practice on within walking distance of home. In the sixth grade, I joined the Flying Eagles ski jumping club. The Flying Eagles was a citywide club of jumpers of all ages who competed in tournaments throughout Wisconsin, Michigan, and Minnesota.

To practice jumping, I had to take the city bus across town to the Fourth Ward ski jump after supper on weeknights or on Saturdays and Sundays. The Fourth Ward jump was lighted until 10:00 PM. Back then, it was no big deal to take our big jumping skis on the city bus, especially when we got the father of future Olympic star Billy Olson as our bus driver. After jumping, we'd either take our skis home or stash them at the Standard gas station next to the jump.

This jump was rather small with a fifty-foot jump being good distance, and that was plenty far enough for me. Once I made too short of a jump and dug my ski tips into the top of the knoll, and I belly flopped down to the bottom knocking the wind out of me. Somebody asked how I was, but I couldn't answer because I had no breath in my lungs. It was so frustrating. I could mouth the words, but no sounds came out.

A lot of people outside the sport don't know how fast one advances in the sport of ski jumping. You start out small by building a jump about a foot high on a fairly steep hill, and you keep adding to the jump making it bigger, which enables longer jumps.

In ski jumping contests, the competitors are judged on distance and form. The jumpers come down the scaffold in a crouched position, and when they reach the end of the scaffold or runway, they spring up and out with all the strength they have in their legs and lean forward floating out with either their arms in front or with their hands placed on their hips; either way is quite stylish. When they land on the knoll in good form, their skis are parallel of course with one ski about eight inches ahead of the other, sometimes called a telemark position. The whole ride down the scaffold, the jump and the landing knoll takes about three seconds. Within about one season, a kid could expect to jump at least sixty feet. A nice custom is the other jumpers waiting their turn at the top of the scaffold say to the jumper just leaving the launching area encouragements like, "Good luck, make it a good one, or hit it." Of course, that means to time your lift off at the end of the scaffold at just the optimum split second to get the right lift for your effort. One can jump like crazy and get very little distance if one jumps too soon or too late. When you finally get that perfect snap off the jump and you feel that second of float and air pressure against your skis and chest, it's a very rare feeling words can't describe.

When we didn't have the time to travel to a regular jump with a scaffold, we built our own jumps. Mostly my friend Bernie Behlke and I used a jump built by Ron Erlandson and Denny Welch down by the Eau Claire River. This jump was rather unusual in that it had a good long slope down to the jump, a steep stretch to land on, a knoll, a short flat stretch, then another knoll, and finally a smooth slope to end the jump on. There was a little problem at the bottom of the landing hill where it flattened out because the jumper had to stop on a dime or he would careen over the ridge into the trees and ultimately wind up in the river a hundred feet below. Needless to say that is how I learned to stop on skis. Thank goodness none of us landed in the drink.

Ron was kind of a sneaky prankster. A couple times when I turned my back and lugged my skis up to the top of the hill, Ron built what we called a kicker on the jump. A kicker was accomplished by adding snow to the jump. Because the kicker made the jump bigger, it would either send the jumper higher or provide surprisingly more horizontal distance to their jump. Once the jumper starts his decent, approaching the jump, there was no stopping because each ski was in a deep groove and of course the skier is going at high speed. Also, the added kicker blended right in with the white snow of the jump, so it was never noticed until it was too late.

One ride down the slope I'll never forget. I wanted to end the day with a new distance record. My start was very aggressive as I gained good speed down the run not noticing the kicker, so when I hit it, I shot straight up vertically farther than I went out horizontally. Flying so high in the air, I actually scraped my head on some overhanging branches of an oak tree close to the first landing knoll. I landed with such a clatter just a few feet from the front of the jump, thinking surely, I had broken every bone in my back. I finished the ride in a daze and looked back at guilty Ron laughing his head off.

One time I left for home and told Ron I would be back early the next morning, probably before anyone else. Sneaky Ron and Denny (who lived next to the jump) got some buckets of water and iced the runway down to the jump. The next morning, I arrived at the jump from the top end of the hill, through the vacant lot next to Welch's house. From my vantage point, I couldn't tell that the runway had been iced. I put my skis on and started down the hill. The immediate high speed alarmed me as I approached the jump in a panic but couldn't stop; it was too late to fall so I just decided to ride it out without jumping. As I rocketed off the end of the jump, I only remember saying out loud, "Jesus Christ!!" And I sailed out so fast, my heart stopped. I thought surely I wouldn't survive this one. I bounced off the first and second knoll and landed on the flat. Fear came over me because I thought I wouldn't be able to stop and might sail off the cliff into the river. It flashed in my mind that if I'm lucky, I'll get tangled in and saved by the poplar and white birth trees. Gritting my teeth and closing my eyes, I swerved to a stop right at the edge. Up to this time the distance record was 27 feet. Surely, I had set the new distance record, but how would I prove it. I vowed to get even with those nitwits that iced the track.

Another goofy ski jump was built by Leroy (Ming) Anderson and Rollie Jacobs. Ming called me one Saturday morning and said, "Yogi, Rollie and I built a really neat ski jump on the steep hill near the Highway 53 bridge. Come over and try it."

I arrived at the jump with high expectations. The jump was impressive all right, but highly unorthodox. They had constructed this one with a nice steep normal runway down to the jump, but the problem was that there was a huge gap (no ground) between the jump and the landing hill. If you did not soar far enough, you just plain crashed into a wall.

Talk about a leap of faith. I took one look and asked, "How did you nuts come up with this idea?"

Rollie said, "Yah isn't it neat? It will keep the little kids off our jump."

"We'll kill ourselves," I told them.

They said, "We already made the distance yesterday. Let's see you do it."

Feeling a little weak, I gulped and thought, "What have I gotten into, and how do I get out of it?" Basically, I trusted Ming and Rollie, so I would try it.

Ming volunteered, "The nice thing about it is that there is no choice. You just plain must make it over the gap or else. It sort of guarantees your best effort. You'd be surprised how that works. You're forced into it."

Putting my skis over my shoulder, I walked up to the top of the hill. I was nervous but thought if I hit the end of the jump with just enough umph, I could get the lift to clear the gap and land on the knoll. Off I go with a strong push sailing down the runway in the usual crouch, and when I hit the jump, I sprang up and forward with perfect leaning. I knew I'd really nailed

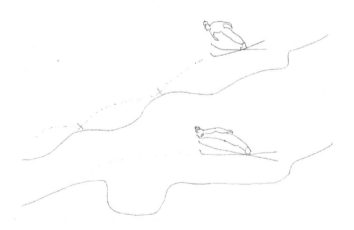

it as I cleared the gap by about six feet. We jumped the rest of the morning and felt good that we were jumping a real novel, custom ski jump.

All in all, ski jumping thrilled me as I got better. To me this was big time stuff, as I had entered a whole 'nother world but much later than the real aces of my town. I knew I'd never be a top jumper, but I loved the sport, and I was proud to be known as a ski jumper at school. To show that we were jumpers, many of us wore our ski boots to school as well as our black knit jumpers' caps, which had a one-inch horizontal white strip and a white pom-pom on top. I usually never wore it centered on my head but jauntily slanted to one side leaning toward one eye.

HALF MOON LAKE

Returning to Half Moon Lake brings back fond memories of Dad teaching me to fish. This well named lake shaped like a half moon is located in the center of beautiful Eau Claire. Half Moon has an island in the middle with a historic logging museum, two city parks with swimming beaches, and a baseball stadium where Hank Aaron played minor league baseball. Most important for Dad and me was Half Moon was the best panfish lake in the area. How can I begin to count the memorable hours of fishing for sunfish, (bluegills) perch, bullheads, and crappies with Dad?

Dad wasn't a fashionable fisherman in the late 1940's. He owned no sports or leisure clothes such as Bermuda shorts or short sleeve sport shirts and no sunglasses. Dad wore old street or business clothes to garden and fish in. He donned an old Stetson hat, worn out wing tip shoes (usually cracked), white dress shirts with frayed collars, and pants worn thin at the knees.

Dad stayed with the basics in techniques and tackle. For bait, we used angleworms dug from the garden. He said after a rain was always good for digging worms because the worms came closer to the surface to seek the fresh moistness in the dirt. We'd get out the spade, an empty Hills Bros.

60

coffee can, and gather angleworms. A real bonus for Dad was when we'd find some thick white grub worms. I can hear him touting, "Nothing catches sunfish like grub worms."

After every rainfall, Dad and I would try to go fishing. I remember going to him as he was reading his Philatelic catalogue on the front porch and saying, "Looks like the rain has ended. Ya know it's time to head for Half Moon." Dad said rain washed worms and terrestrials into the water from the soil, grasses, and tree leaves along the shore which would trigger a feeding frenzy among opportune fish. Sure enough, we always did well after a rain.

Mother would make us a lunch and put it in a brown paper bag. We never had an official metal lunch bucket. I figured if you didn't work at a factory, you didn't use one.

The standard fare was peanut butter, Spam, or egg salad sandwiches with chocolate chip cookies and a banana. Mom would throw in a bottle of Coke for me, and Dad made up coffee for his plain steel thermos.

My anticipation went wild when we got to the Half Moon Lake boat livery. I loved this old livery where all the wooden boats had about a dozen coats of green paint, and some of them leaked. The boats sat in water under a wood canopy, and in every one was an empty coffee can for bailing water. The boat rental must have been cheap because Dad never complained.

No outboard motor for us. We'd row to beat the band to what looked like a good spot. Dad was very insistent about fishing near lily pads or old tree stumps sticking out of the water. He said, "Anywhere there is something the fish can hide by is good." He said, "You see, the big fish such as northern pike are always lurking around trying to eat the sunfish, so the sunnies need a hiding place."

With our worms, we used cane poles, real cork we made into bobbers, and black line tied directly to the hook. I wondered if using clear catgut line on the end of the black line might fool more fish. Dad pooh-poohed that notion.

Once my heart sank when I reached into the Hills Bros. coffee can and discovered we were out of worms. Dad said, "No sweat, we'll use fisheyes." To my astonishment, he grabbed a fish from off our stringer,

61

took the hook, and with the proficiency of a surgeon, extracted the eyeball leaving a clean eye socket. Dad said, "Actually, Bill, there's nothing better than fisheyes for catching sunfish. The eyes are tough, so you don't have to keep re-baiting your hook." Sure enough, the fisheyes worked like crazy. I had a good laugh over this resourceful way of catching fish.

No store-bought stringer for us. We used a piece of rope from the garage. One time when we had the rope hanging over the side of the boat, a bunch of turtles started chomping on our fish. Dad said he'd show them. So the next time, he used a mesh potato bag but got the same results.

Dad had great patience. After rowing to some likely looking spot and anchoring, we'd sit there for the longest time waiting for a bite. If I suggested moving, he'd just say, "They're here but just not biting yet. Ya just have to wait for 'em." Getting a little bored waiting for a bite, I'd start eating lunch. Lunches were stored in the shady part of the boat, which meant they were under the seat on the floor of the boat. Of course, the lunches would get wet. I asked him what difference it made to store the lunches in the shade on a day with the temps in the 70's and 80's, and he would say it is better than nothing. I suggested we stop by the sporting goods section of the Sears Roebuck store and check out the coolers. Coolers were the newest thing, and ice in the coolers would keep our lunches cool and dry. To him that was just a foolish luxury. What a joy to dig sandwiches and cookies out of wet wax paper. By then the Coke was warm of course.

Even back in the forties, I felt that we looked like something out of the past. A lot of the fishermen had motorboats, wore waders or hip boots, and used fly rods and wicker creels. With Dad though, we did it his way because he said his method worked, and it sort of did. We always caught fish for supper. Even our fishing poles were goofy looking. We'd start the season with ten-foot long willowy cane poles we bought at the Rod and Gun Sport Shop, but soon they'd break from being stashed in the corner of the garage or by the car door. Dad would just saw the broken tip off and rig it up again. By the end of one season, my rod was about four feet (thick stub with no flex), and his was six feet long. I felt so self-conscious being seen with such amateurish equipment. Much to my disappointment, Dad didn't replace those rods the following year.

It never ceased to amaze me how every time Dad caught a fish, it seemed like it was the first fish he ever caught. He was like a kid, thrilled and so proud. I wondered about that — him getting more excited about catching fish than me. I can still hear him say, "Bill you've got a nibble. Let him take it. It's still nibbling, let him take it. When he takes the bobber about four inches under the water, then pull up."

When there was a pause in the action, I used to look over at him as he smoked his pipe with a small cloud of smoke drifting off into the air, and next to him on the boat seat the familiar blue pocket sized tin of Grangers pipe tobacco with the yellow letters, MILD-FRAGRANT-COOL. He would have a distant, frozen in time, contented look on his face. To me it looked like he was reconnecting with his father, fishing this same way on good old Half Moon Lake.

One day Ron Erlandson asked me if Dad and I wanted to go fishing with him and his dad. That is when I did something I regretted the entire summer. I told Ron I was embarrassed about the simple way my Dad fished. I said, "Ron, Dad is strictly a worm dunker and doesn't understand the way you guys use modern fly-fishing equipment." Plus, I said, "Dad gets overly excited when he catches a fish, and he's like a little kid." Later I realized my father overheard that conversation because there was a chilly distance between us the rest of the day. His feelings were hurt, and I never forgot that feeling of shame the entire summer.

Besides the Erlandson's having all the equipment for fly-fishing and using casting rods, Reverend King up the alley was well equipped with his own boat and outboard motor. Other families in the neighborhood had lake cabins. I'd bug Dad about getting a cabin on a lake, he'd just say, "Why get a lake cabin when we catch all the fish we need at Half Moon Lake?"

With our meager funds, some of us junior high school guys bought used fly rods and stashed them in our school lockers in May so we could fish Half Moon (four blocks away) after school hours. My rod was a three-piece bamboo Montague Sun Beam. In early May, the crappies were easy to catch as they spawned first right up near the shoreline. In late May, the bluegills spawned so we would have a blast catching them. If we didn't have our wicker creels with us, we'd put the fish in mesh potato bags and bring them home on the bus. We laid the smelly bags of fish on the center floor of the bus, and the ladies riding the bus would offer to buy our fish. We never sold.

Decades later I still return to Half Moon Lake. In May, I go back to Eau Claire to plant flowers around my parents' graves at Lake View Cemetery which overlooks Half Moon Lake. After planting the graves, I walk over to the ridge above the lake, and on a clear, calm day with a high sun and using my polarized glasses, I peer down into the water far below and see male bluegills suspended in the water staging their move to come in to set up spawning beds. A week or so later, the female bluegills move from the depths to join the males, and the nuptials begin. I try to time my visits so I don't catch the females while they're spawning, because I hate to thwart the laying of thousands of valuable eggs and the males fertilizing the eggs. Mostly I catch and release.

After I wade into the water and catch just enough for one meal, I walk back to the cemetery and go to my Dad's grave to have a little chat. Placing my fly rod and creel next to his grave, I thank him for taking me fishing. "By the way Dad, your favorite wildflower, the Snow Trillium, is out in its full glory — some almost the size of baseballs." His spirit is present, and I recall the fun and togetherness fishing Half Moon gave us. I tell him that he had it right, that fishing is about recreation, keeping it simple, and not about how many fish or new-fangled equipment. For Dad, contentment was enough. "Thanks Dad. It's because of you that I am now a lifetime fisherman, and I have passed the tradition onto my children. That brings me great joy."

TRICKS OR TREATS

This is a great Halloween neighborhood. I've said it often when I pass through a part of town where there are old houses with spires and cracked sidewalks shrouded by bushes leading to front porches. And of course, old trees with black branches in the front yard and dark alleys. The thick atmosphere just made for spooky nights.

Lo and behold in second or third grade I won the best costume contest wearing my oldest overalls, worn thin flannel shirt, Dad's oldest fedora hat, leather boots, small black mask, and a knapsack tied to the pole mother used to stir clothes in the stationary tub. My prize was the classroom Jack-O-Lantern.

I got the idea for this bum/hobo outfit from Mother. She had a *thing* about bums down by the river. She'd tell me they'd get off the train cars, cook meals over fires, sleep in caves, and drink Sterno canned heat to get drunk. She warned they might snatch me. Well, that sounded very exciting to me, so when I'd go to the river, I'd search very hard to spy on these bums. In all my forays I saw nary a bum.

Against my parents' advice, I chose to take my pumpkin tricks or treating. So with Dad's help, I stuck a candle in melted wax inside the pumpkin. Dad lit the candle. I was set with my mighty Jack-O-Lantern.

Again Mom and Dad tried heartily to discourage me from taking it out. I was half nuts waiting for it to get dark.

With my best friend Tommy Benson, big brother Bob, and Ron Erlandson, we set out. Surely, I'd be a star tonight with an authentic Jack-O-Lantern. So 'course I was, except at the first house I dropped it with a thud on the front porch, splitting it wide open and putting out the candle. My spirits weren't dashed as I scampered home and grabbed toothpicks to stick in the crack of my pumpkin to sew it up.

Dad said the pumpkin, sack for candy, and my hobo's pole with knapsack was too much to manage. Their advice fell on deaf ears. On this night, I wanted to be a *standout.* So off I went to catch up with the others. Refreshed, I proudly went to a couple more houses and got praises from the treat givers. Other kids stopped to admire it, but then one big bozo slapped my lantern, and it plopped on the sidewalk as the kid ran away. To my disappointment, Ron and Bob didn't set out in pursuit of him.

So back home for more toothpick patching. Now Mom and Dad got rather stern with me, but I was possessed and ran out the door. I ran like crazy to catch up with the guys, and Ron suggested we take the alley from Summer Street to Chauncey Street. I said, "NO! Not tonight." I can't count the times I walked in pitch darkness down that alley. But for sure it was too spooky tonight. After all, it was Halloween. There could be older rascals waxing windows and tipping over garbage cans in backyards. Then Ron shouted, "Follow the deer trail." Bob, Ron, and Tommy headed down the alley, singing, "Star light, star bright. Hope to see the witch tonight," messing with me about how brave they were.

I went on alone to two more houses, and I dropped my pumpkin again, splitting it in half. Totally exasperated, I headed home and dumped it in the insinuator or maybe the garbage can and went in the house. I didn't even spread my candy out on the dining room table or living room floor. I immediately hit the hay, asleep before my head hit the pillow. The next morning Bob told me he caught holy hell for leaving me alone out there last night.

The Barlands

WAR OF MY YOUTH

We kids knew there was a war on but it became more real when our teacher Miss Brotman invited her soldier boy to our class. On that spring day in fourth grade, our Eau Claire Second Ward grade schoolteacher looked a little prettier than usual in her black dress with white polka dots, puffy shoulder pads and narrow shiny black leather belt. Her demeanor was different as she kept glancing at our classroom wall clock. Suddenly at 10:00 there was a knock on the door, and she flew out of her chair heading for the door. Opening the door, she let out a slight squeak and disappeared momentarily and then reappeared with a soldier on her arm. With a look of genuine pride, she said, "Class, this is Lloyd Thompson, my soldier boy. We're engaged to be married." She added, "Lloydy, this is my wonderful class. I'm so proud of all my students. Students, Lloydy knows all about you from my letters."

We were so surprised when we heard she was proud of us and even wrote about us to her boyfriend in the war. We looked at each other half blushing, half smiling. She went on to say that in her letters she told him all about us taking on handwriting, expanding our reading, and arithmetic. She also said, "Remember children how I told you that in Lloydy's letters to me he often couldn't tell me exactly where he was in Germany because if the Germans

67

somehow discovered the letter, they would know exactly where our soldiers were." Wow, we students were so impressed with how it all was so big and secretive.

Our teacher said, "Did any of you notice that I'm wearing a diamond engagement ring? Lloydy gave it to me Saturday night." Not one of us had noticed her ring. Our teacher held up her left hand and said, "If you would like, you can form a line and come up to see my diamond ring."

We did, but it sure looked small to me. I couldn't see a glitter, which sort of embarrassed me, so I said, "Yah, that's really neat." Eleanor Gilbertson told me she saw the little diamond with a sparkle.

Miss Brotman said, "Lloyd is on furlough for a couple weeks."

Gretchen Schultz raised her hand and asked, "Are you going to get married real soon"?

Miss Brotman responded, "We hope so, but we don't know exactly when. It depends on when we win the war."

Tommy Benson piped up, "What's a what's-a-ma-call-it? What's the word you used?"

Miss Brotman said, "Do you mean what's a furlough?"

"Yah," a couple of us said.

"Well," she said, "A furlough is a vacation from the war service. You know soldiers need a vacation, too. I will write the word on the blackboard. Now let's all say F-U-R-L-O-U-G-H." We did, very slowly and in unison. She added, "It is kind of a hard word, but someday you will learn to spell these big words."

Janet Schreiber stood up and asked Lloyd about the patches on his uniform. Somebody else asked if the pins and gold trim on his uniform were real gold.

Lloyd said, "No, no it's metal with a gold colored coating."

Again, Miss Brotman interjected, "This may be a good time for Lloyd to tell about his uniform."

But Roddy Monson asked if he had a jeep and did he sleep in a foxhole.

Lloyd said he rode in a jeep once in awhile, and he slept in a barracks but had spent a lot of time in foxholes. He said, "Foxholes are terrible places, full of water and mud, and no place to sleep. They are dangerous because that's where a lot of soldiers get killed by the Germans."

Raising my hand, I got the nod and asked, "How many Germans did you shoot?"

Our teacher said, "Wait a second, please children, let's not ask about killing. Remember Lloyd is on furlough. We know that furlough is a break from war, even talking about war, if the soldier chooses."

At that point Lloyd said, "It's OK, I'll just say this, that yes, I have shot at the enemy, but I don't know if or how many Germans I've killed. Maybe none. Not sure I want to know." All us kids kind of understood that he had probably killed somebody, but it was something he doesn't brag about, which was a disappointment to us!

By this time, Lloydy was sitting in Miss Brotman's seat behind her desk, and Miss Brotman was standing right behind him. She must have sensed his tenseness, so she placed her hands on his shoulders. In three motions in one, she patted, squeezed, and caressed his shoulders in such a sweet, calming way. I will never forget that.

To me Lloyd looked so handsome and gallant in his uniform. Lloyd stood up and asked, "Would you like me to explain my uniform to you?"

We jumped out of our seats and shouted, "Yes!" We kids looked at each other with that certain look that we are really getting in on something special.

The uniform was all brown. The coat came down over his waist and had a belt with a shiny gold buckle. There were several colorful horizontal patches on the left side of his chest, and he explained how each color represented a country where he served, U.S.A, England, France, and Germany. The upside-down gold **V** shaped patches on his left sleeve just below his left shoulder showed what his rank was in the Army.

Geraldine Phillips asked, "How come your shoes are so shiny?" Lloyd went on to explain about spit shining he learned in boot camp.

Herman Manthei, grimaced and said, "Spit shining?"

Lloyd asked, "Would you like me to pass my hat around the room?" He didn't need to ask. We marveled at the shiny leather bill with a strap in front that had gold fasteners with eagle imprints. Lloyd ended by demonstrating how to salute and explained its meaning.

I loved looking at Miss Brotman as she adoringly watched Lloyd. She had natural beauty with a dark complexion, slim statuesque athletic figure, and an outdoorsy look. She barely used any facial makeup. It became clear to us that Lloyd and our teacher were very much in love, and we liked that. Miss Brotman went from a very controlled, efficient, and composed woman to a relaxed, less guarded girl. She had a glow about her, and we had never seen her smile and laugh so much. This was the first time I can say I saw the look of love, and it was in our teacher's movements and eyes. The thing that sticks in my mind is that we students were invited into her joy that day. Lloyd quickly became our hero. By golly it was unanimous. This soldier boy was the only person good enough for our teacher.

After hearing all about uniforms and military life, we were given an assignment, which was designed to keep us very busy at our desk so the two of them could talk. It didn't do much good, as we couldn't keep our eyes off the two sweethearts. Not that we thought we would see them kiss, but maybe hold hands or something. Every time I looked up at them, she would give me that, back to your assignment Billy look with a sweet understanding smile. All I knew was that I loved that morning and Edna Brotman.

I also thought about how much I wanted a soldier uniform. In my home, we had both the Sears Roebuck and Montgomery Ward catalogs. There were several pages of uniforms for kids that one could mail order. It seemed like I paged through this section daily, mostly zeroing in on army uniforms. I asked Santa with no luck, and my birthday brought me disappointment. My parents said these uniforms are too expensive and I would grow out of one too soon.

Personally, the war didn't affect me much, except for the loss of bubble gum. My oldest brother told me that it was because bubble gum had rubber in it (that's what makes it stretch to create the bubble), and the army needed more rubber to make tires for their jeeps. That made sense to me. I remember just before the bubble gum ran out at Ma Shafer's market, she limited one piece of gum to each customer so every kid would get a piece.

I remember how my dad bought gas masks for our family. He said, "Because here in Eau Claire we have the Gillette Tire Company plant and the National Presto Industries munitions plant in our town, we could be a big target for a German bomb if they ever got this far." It seemed like every other Sunday night Dad would haul these goofy looking gas masks out of the closet to demonstrate how to use them in case of an air raid. Even at the age of seven, I had my doubts the Germans would ever reach Eau Claire because Lloyd Thompson assured us that would never happen.

A few months after Lloyd visited our class, I was walking down to Boyd Park after supper when the Gillette Tire Co. plant siren started blaring and all the church bells clanged. I knew in that instant WWII was over, and I got a warm feeling in my heart that our soldier boys would come home, and Miss Brotman and Lloyd would marry soon. Knowing the war had ended, I sensed I should go home to be with my family. I passed a few houses on our block with small American flags in windows indicating that someone from that household was serving in the war. One grieving home had a gold star in the window. Arriving at my house, I saw the Carlsons next door on their front porch with the American flag, and they were in tears. I asked Mom why they were crying, and she said, "It's because their son Brule will be coming home from the war. Those were tears of joy." Those kinds of tears were new to me.

A special additional note about World War II:

It turns out that one of our classmates, Gordan Barland, was present during the bombing of Pearl Harbor. Gordan remembered three waves of roars in the sky. Looking up he saw airplanes with red circles on the bottom of the wings indicating they were Japanese aircraft. Gordy peddled his trike to safety.

LAUREL MISSISSIPPI

My grandfather Hans Solberg was my most colorful relative, and he died before I was born. Every time I was sick as a child, I would ask my mother to sit on the edge of my bed and tell me stories about the south. The stories showed how bright and adventurous her father was and how he came to America from Norway to seize the American dream of getting rich. Settling in Eau Claire Hans was inspired by the logging barons three storied houses with spires and widow watches. So grandiose to my grandfather.

Mother claimed her father was the best millwright in the logging community of Eau Claire. Hans' specialty was making failing logging mills profitable. He was so highly regarded by his company that they sent him to their newest venture, a start-up plant in Laurel, Mississippi.

Hans went to the steamy south to get things set up for his family. Then he sent for his mother, wife and three daughters. They moved into a house on stilts. Stilted houses were common in those parts near the logging operations to keep snakes from entering the homes. It wasn't long before Hans announced, "Our girls will not attend southern schools, they'll get their education in the better schools up north." So back to Eau Claire they went, everyone except Hans.

My wish has always been to visit Laurel, Mississippi to see if I can find any traces of this man's life. When I arrive in Faulkner country, I'd be anxious to visit the public library's archival system in Laurel to see if there are any old photos and books of the original logging days around that part of Mississippi. Maybe there's an outside chance of a picture or mention in a book about individual bosses or milling gangs where I might get a clue.

Hans made a good salary for the early nineteen hundreds, and he was known as a lucky gambler around Laurel. Saturday nights were gambling nights at the local watering holes. Hans won and used his gambling earnings to speculate in Oklahoma oil. The oil companies would always alert him that they were very close but needed more money to drill down to the mother-load. Hans always sent the money but lost on the scams.

My grandfather had what was called a "crew of prison and jail convicts" that catered to his every whim. He also carried a pearl handled pistol, which was a status symbol among the crew bosses. Those must have been wild and wooly days in those logging towns in the deep south.

Hans asked his wife, Josephine, if he could bring his favorite convict, Willy Smith to Eau Claire for a visit. Josephine said, "Hans, you will not bring a convict to Eau Claire."

Besides work, gambling, and drinking, Hans and his buddies hunted alligators for sport. These men made beautiful belts, purses, and shoes out of alligator skin. Hans sent these prized items back to Eau Claire for his family and said, "Alligator hide lasts forever."

Occasionally Hans would take the train north to visit his family in Eau Claire. He arrived with watermelons smothered in ice. The only request to his wife was that when he got there she'd have two cases of Walter's beer waiting on the back porch.

After an early retirement grandpa spent an entire summer traipsing through Norway visiting relatives. He was welcomed as sort of a hero for making it big in America. Every farm he visited served him farm fresh cream based meals. When he returned from his trip my mother went to pick him up at the Eau Claire train depot and walked right by him twice without recognizing him because he had gained so much weight. Later that year

Hans went to Seattle, Washington to visit his brother and while returning home on the train he suffered five strokes and died.

In recent years I have often thought about how my grandfather's free spirit lifestyle and long absences from his family affected his daughter's choices in husbands. Even though my mother was a woman of high spirit, intelligence, imagination, and energy, she picked a stiff tea-totaler accountant, the consummate conservative. My aunt Grace wound up with a dairy farmer who was a pillar in their small town and who loved farming and delivering milk. Aunt Mae never bothered much with men. She remained single and once said, "Men are for the birds." These sisters never used alcohol except Mae loved occasional Manhattans while dining out.

My mother and her sisters were driven people. They decided to break the mold by having their own careers so they could control their destinies. Starting in Junior High School all three girls had jobs after school. At the earliest opportunities these sisters got teaching certificates from Eau Claire State Teachers College. They felt strongly that it was up to them to make it in the world, and all three had very successful careers in the education field.

Aunt Grace and my mother always pushed their sons and nephews to get a good education in order to achieve social and economic security at a high level. I feel there was always that overriding issue of insecurity caused by an absentee father in my mother and my aunts. I can hear mother say, "It's up to nobody but yourself."

About fifty-five years ago a guy in my coffee group, who was married to a girl from Laurel, MS., said he'd ask about Hans when he and his wife went back to Laurel for a visit. He asked several old timers, some in their nineties that said, "Oh sure, good ol' Hans, he was a rounder." But, my friend said, "These old timers like to tell you things they think you want to hear, like them knowing him. You can't put much stock in it, they probably never knew him, you'll never know."

I think about what traits Hans passed on to his grandson's. My oldest brother, Jon, inherited Hans' talent for reviving failing businesses. My other brother, Bob, got my grandfather's bent toward gaming and the high life. Me, I guess I got my grandfather's love of hunting, fishing and the great outdoors. Hans was truly a big figure with huge spirit, intelligence, and energy — a true adventurer.

Forty years ago, I got totally immersed in Henrik Ibsen's epoch play Peer Gynt by reading the book and attending the play at the Guthrie Theater in Minneapolis. I went to the pre-play lecture put on by Hy Berman. Hy Berman was a retired University of Minnesota history professor. Prof. Berman gave a great talk that explained all the historical, social and political implications of this great play. How those dreamers like Hans Solberg left their homeland and went to other countries and rode the capitalist wave and then returned to visit their native Norway. Some genuine successes and some half-baked successes. This whole Guthrie experience helped me better understand my colorful grandfather and it spurred me on to find out more about this Peer Gynt wannaby.

BROOKIES

Eastern Brook Trout, (Salvelinus frontinalus), are revered in northcentral Wisconsin. Some called them Speckled Trout. These indigenous native Trout are born in the highest quality steams and have the prettiest colors. Their salmon colored meat is considered the best.

Avid Brookie anglers are in an anticipatory fervor, barely able to sleep, waiting for dawn of opening day. Most know where to go. They have secret spots they never disclosed outside their family — just like morel mushroom hunters.

I love the Ojibwa and French names of Trout streams such as Weirgor, Pemebonwon, Bois Brule River and Couderay to name a few. Actually, I also love the names of feeder streams like Soft Maple (really engaging name) that flows into the Weirgor. A real treasure is to know of a Beaver damn where Brookies were bunched up making them easier to catch because they couldn't scatter up or down stream.

There are other Trout in our streams such as Rainbow and German Brown Trout. The Rainbows were dumped in streams by hatchery trucks, and the Browns that were originally foreign, were established in some waters decades before by the Wisconsin Department of Natural Resources.

The Browns reproduced and flourished but didn't eat as well, nor did the Rainbows.

Some streams are close to Eau Claire, but most are hours away usually "Up North." Quite a group of anglers drive to the far off destinations on Friday nights. Our local Otter Creek once had a good population of Brookies, but there was a lot of fishing pressure, so the population of Brook Trout diminished and left only smaller Trout in the upper reaches of the crick near the cold springs.

The Bernhardt Behlkes were a Trout fishing family of five. They'd travel way up to Delta, WI. to fish the White River, Bolens, Fish and Pine Creeks. Bernhardt Sr. bought the first Nash car model that featured collapsible seats for sleeping four people. Little sis had to find a nook to snuggle in.

One Monday, I stopped by to see Bernie Jr., and I was invited into the kitchen where Mrs. Behlke was frying Trout for breakfast in a huge pan. She showed me and described the Trout. She said, "See these with the pinkish orange meat? They are native Brook Trout — the best eating Trout. These two are stocked Rainbow Trout — not so good — and these are Browns — just fair eating. It's the Brookies we seek, but we're not into throwing any Trout back into the stream."

Later that day, Junior and I decided to fish the Eau Claire River with crayfish. Junior said, "My dad has a night crawler pen next to our goldfish pond."

I said, "What? What's a night crawler pen?"

He said, "A wooden crate sunk into the ground and filled with dirt for the giant worms to live. The giant ten-inch earth worms come out at night, always after a rain, onto the grass of city parks, golf courses, and cemeteries. We use a flashlight to see them when they appear out of the ground. We make sure the light isn't directly on them, so they don't scoot back into the hole. Then we quickly grab them. We bring then back in a can with a little dirt and dump them into the dirt filled wooden crate. We fish so much we need a ready supply because the bait shops often run out of crawlers."

I asked, "How the heck do you feed them?" Bernie answered, "Just some sort of itty-bitty food scraps

"Beats me how that works, but good chance they find food in the dirt we don't know about."

This sport of fishing is imprinted on my mind. I grew up thinking the stream Trout fly fishers were the highest level of anglers and biggest in numbers. I still remember them with a bamboo fly rod, hip boots, wicker creel, and hat with flies attached. The old timers were a breed of their own — totally dedicated. I wanted to find their enchanting Brook Trout haunts.

MANLEY MONSON

My childhood on Eau Claire's east side hill was idyllic and innocent. I was shocked when I learned that the Monson family across the alley was dysfunctional. Years after we moved from Eau Claire to Minneapolis, Dad announced that the father, Manley Monson, used to be an alcoholic. He may have been one of the earliest Alcoholic Anonymous members because we only saw him sober.

Some lessons in life are shocking to a young kid, and one day I saw just how scary family life can be. I saw Manley chasing his wife through their backyard, crossing the alley, and ending at the big oak tree next to our garage. She was carrying a bank check in her fist, and Mr. Monson, looking mean, used his physical strength to pin her against the tree. Mrs. Monson screamed, "I want the money, you fool. I need some things."

They struggled, and she started crying. He seized the check. Never, never had I ever imagined that married people fought like that. It made me sick to my stomach as I ran into our house.

This dysfunctional family put some scars on son Rodney. The older sister Audrey didn't seem affected by the stress. She went to Macalester College in St. Paul, Minnesota, graduated Summa Cum Laude, and had a successful career as a social worker.

Rod attended St. Olaf College in Northfield, MN. and was a part-time disk jockey on the college radio station. He started having social problems and dropped out of college. Roddy was an odd duck. Eventually, he drifted out to Montana and got a job at a small-town radio station. There was word that Roddy's problems with alcohol and his loopy behavior kept him from holding down a job.

Eventually, Rod returned to Eau Claire in his late thirties or early forties and perished, with his girlfriend, in a fire that burned down the bar where they lived upstairs. A very sad ending.

THERE'S MORE

Manley was the Safety Supervisor for Northern States Power Co. He took it seriously.

One day when Roddy Monson, Donny Burns, and I were playing cars in a sandy area next to Donny's garage, Mr. Monson came to us with a proposal.

This was when Eau Claire was on a safety kick about reckless young bikers. The city decided to select certain kids to sort of monitor other young bikers. The patrol kids were given authority to pull over reckless bikers and tell them to shape up then give out the bike safety brochure. The patrol monitors were given metal badges to show their authority.

Manley told us we should take this venture even further. He said we should start saving our money, so we'd have enough to build a cart with a real motor to patrol the streets. We bought the idea hook, line, and sinker. Wow! We'd be super patrollers! Manley said we could probably buy enough material to build a cart with a little over $100.00. Mr. Monson said he'd talk to the safety supervisor for the city to get the OK. Donny, Roddy and I started dreaming with great resolve to save enough to build this glorious patrol cart.

I, of course, very excitedly told my parents of our future high status with the cart. Dad just sort of blew it off.

Time went by, and we talked and dreamed of glory. We used a tin box of Rod's as our bank and stashed it in Monson's garage. Occasionally Manley would ask how we're doing, and we gave him good reports in the early stages. After four months, we might have had as much as $3.00. Our dream fizzled out.

MOTHER'S COOKING

The wonderful smell of vanilla enticed me to finger my way through mother's old wooden recipe box — a trip conjuring up fond memories of family gatherings. The wood box was well varnished, but the hinges were loose, and the top was hanging by one hinge. Her maiden name, Irene M. Solberg, was painted on the top.

I chuckled as I saw how she altered recipes. The Sunshine Pie (lemon) card calls for one teaspoon of vanilla, but she added more. On the lemon concentrate, she crossed out the one and wrote, "But I use two teaspoons." Her chocolate pie recipe called for one teaspoon of vanilla, but she crossed out the one and added another half teaspoon, and she snuck extra sugar into some cookie recipes. Mother always tried to give a dessert recipe more umph.

The pie section is by far the largest — which explains why there is a card taped to the outside front of the recipe box for Crisco pie crust — you can't miss it. Several of the pie and cookie recipes were from Mom's friends. A little note on one card, "Yummy, Irene," from Hanna, and "You'll get praises from Nan Tilleson and Marion Bennett on this sandbakkel recipe."

Apparently, chocolate was my mother's favorite pie because there were four cards for chocolate pie. On one of the cards, she increased the recipe by 50%. When mother did the math on this card, she wasn't thinking about including more eaters. It was about bigger portions per eater. Instead of the chocolate pie being 1 inch high, it wound up being 1 ½ inches high. Bigger was better — yummy.

Obviously over the decades, mother didn't follow convention in her cooking because she wanted to please us more. So, her meatballs grew. One day after my college years, I was sitting at my parents' kitchen table having a couple of meatballs when my friend Jack Forrest walked into our house. He looked, laughed, and said, "My goodness, those are big meatballs."

I responded, "My mother makes the best meatballs. Do you want one Jack?"

Jack sat down, shook his head, and said, "These are almost the size of baseballs. A new record. I'd call these country meatballs, or Texas meatballs." I remembered when I was a child her meatballs started out the size of golf balls.

Mother's cooking and baking campaign was lifted to new heights when she got her first chest-style freezer. She marched all her friends and neighbors into the basement to show them her new freezer. She was proud to point out that her freezer was filled to the brim. Ma could always pull something out of the freezer if company was coming. She dang near froze everything except the salt and pepper.

One day in August, I walked into the house to find her baking and decorating Christmas cookies. I didn't think much about it. I just figured oh well, that's Ma baking ahead of schedule and freezing it. She told me that her fellow teachers praised her for getting her Christmas baking done before Thanksgiving. Mother loved the praise.

As I continued flipping through the recipe box, it was obvious that we were mostly a meat, potato, bread, gravy and dessert family. Only occasionally we did have hot dishes and most of them had as their base good old Campbell's cream of mushroom soup. It was hard to believe that there wasn't one recipe card in the vegetable section.

Mother's thoroughness was well known. When I was Mother's helper in the kitchen, she expected perfection from me. In grade school, I'd help with the Norwegian Christmas baking. We'd start about one week before Christmas (before we had the big freezer). I spent hours filling sandbakkel tins with dough. Mother would look over my shoulder and say, "Oh, Willy, that won't do. These are too lumpy in some spots and too thin in other spots. Your little fingers are having a hard time getting the dough evenly in the curves of the tins. Be sure to use enough dough to cover the sides of the tins all the way to the top, then smooth out the top so the sandbakkel doesn't have ragged edges. Here, let me show you how. It just takes practice." Sure enough, she'd make a perfect sandbakklel, and with practice, I got just about as good.

Mother, bless her soul, had a tendency in her advanced years to overcook meat. She'd say, "I think I'll leave the meat in a few more minutes." Those roasts were served so dry that we needed to moisten them with plenty of thick, well-seasoned gravy to help the taste. The gravy didn't do our waistlines and cardiovascular system any good.

I do have fond memories of Mother cooking BBQ hamburgers in the pressure cooker and bringing the meat in a pan wrapped in kitchen towels to the park.

Chilled fruit salads were big with Ma for these big dinners. She would take a can of Del Monte fruit cocktail, mix in banana chunks and whip cream, put the mix in small-stemmed glasses, and freeze them. Usually too late, she'd pull these crystallized salads from the freezer, apply a small dollop of Cool Whip, and plop a maraschino cherry on top. We'd practically bend our forks trying to spear a morsel.

Big, overflowing Lazy Susans occupied the center of the table. Included were celery and carrot sticks, radishes, green and black olives, cottage cheese, sometimes herring, dill pickles, and the ever-popular pickled beets.

My mother mistakenly served my cousin and his Southern wife a ham loaf for dinner. His wife commented afterwards, "It is a sacrilege to serve ground up ham into a loaf!" Southern ham is special and not to be ground up.

Cooking and a well-kept house were Mother's way of displaying love for her family. She even became a food pusher. She would get up from her seat at the dining room table and go around to each person dishing up a second, and if she could get away with it, a third helping.

Ma would admonish me, "If you are going to Boyd Park to play baseball, you'd better eat a big meal." Her favorite saying on cold winter days was, "This meal will stick to your ribs."

I wish I had known back then just how well those meals would stick to my ribs. I might have said, "I'll take more hugs and less waistline Mother dear."

MY BIRCHES

Reading Robert Frost's poem "BIRCHES" brought me back to the time my cousins and I swung on birch tree branches. At times my cousins Jim and Charles Henrickson and I had to create our own fun on their small dairy farm near Cornell. One bluebird day in June, it dawned on me that we should cross their cornfield to the small patch of woods and look for tree limbs to swing on like Tarzan of the jungle. We did this for several hours until we were almost physically spent.

Through trial and error, we selected the perfect trees for this sport. It was the medium growth trees that had the suppleness and strength to carry us from top of the tree to the ground with perfect sweeps. There was an advantage to grab a branch just out of reach. We needed to spring off from a branch with our feet to get that extra six inches to grab the ideal branches. It reminded me of how in August the biggest most beautifully colored apples were just out of reach. Taking that daring reach to grab the best branch made it all the sweeter when we came careening from high up to get that perfect landing.

We went wild swinging on those trees as we chortled like Tarzan. One time, Charles forgot to release at the right time and plopped down with a thud and got the wind knocked out of him. Ten minutes later, Charles got his breath and was back in the game. One time, Jim released too late and was dashed into the edge of a fen and got his feet soaked. I tried for the

85

world record sweep by going out on a branch too thick and found out that it didn't have enough spring, and I was stranded twenty feet up in midair. I made a perilous retreat back to the trunk of the tree. Eventually all three of us became proficient at smooth landings among the plush ferns on the forest floor.

After all of the best branches were bent over and drooping, it was time to head back to the house. We were a scraggly looking bunch in our grass stained bib overalls. We were sweaty, had scratches on our faces and arms, and my eyeglass rims were bent. Fagged out and starved, we trudged, but half-way through the cornfield, we were spurred on by that heavenly smell of Aunt Grace's fresh baked bread cooling on the back porch railing.

Jim said, "Bill, have you ever had home baked bread with butter and lots of sugar on it?"

I said, "No, but that sounds right up my alley."

After the three of us ate three quarters of a loaf of scrumptious bread, Grace shooed us out of the house. I told Jim that that was my new best way to eat fresh baked bread.

A decade later while reading Robert Frost, I came across his "Birches" again. I was jolted. Frost spoke to me in his wonderful poem describing the farm boy swinging on his father's birch trees. I said, "I've been there, I know birches. I was a swinger of birches. My cousins and I were convinced that we discovered this sport. Surely, we invented it we felt, but it looks like the great bard himself may have discovered it as he states in his poem, "So was I once myself a swinger of birches."

A few years later, I returned to that grove of birch in Henrickson's woods to recapture the memory of that perfect tree-swinging day. As I approached the grove, the earthy fragrances of the fresh spring flora lifted my spirit. Naively hoping to find bent over branches, I found the birches had indeed righted themselves and straightened up to full splendor. I was disappointed the birches hadn't remembered the kids who loved them and had so much fun with them that June day. If only some of their branches were still bent over as we had left them, I could have touched and talked to the branches as I dreamed back to the afternoon that is burned in my memory. Of course, Frost had it right when he states in his poem that artificial bending of the branches wouldn't last, only natural events like ice storms can keep the branches permanently bent over.

Often, I have passed by groves of birch and thought how it would do my heart good to see kids swinging, screaming, and laughing as they swished through the air. I love how Robert Frost said it well in the last sentence of his poem, "One could do worse than be a swinger of birches." I received a glorious gift from birch trees, I know **Birches.**

"The woods was our outdoor library." – Toni Bennett Easterson

MY WONDERFUL MAUDE

Of all the sights and people we met on our eastern road trip from Eau Claire to the east coast, the most memorable of all was meeting Maude in Appomattox, Virginia and her incredible hugs. In 1950 Dad picked up our new "Merry Oldsmobile". The next day Mom and Dad announced it was time for the family to hit the road on a long drive. Two ideas were tossed around. I glommed onto Yellowstone Park because I was soooo enamored with cowboys, Indians, antelope, buffalo, ranches, Buffalo Bill Cody Museum, and the Rocky Mountains.

Dang, my hopes were dashed when the powers that be decided on a historical eastern trip. "Get these kids some education." So, the car pointed east.

After the fabulous Blue Ridge Mountains, we arrived at the Civil War site of Appomattox, Virginia. It was impressive I admit, but I also loved hearing the bob white quail's songs from the weed patches.

Dad asked a local guy where we could get a good supper. The southern gent advised we go to Maude's Hot Shop. Maude's featured Southern style cooking. The place was packed. Maude herself came out of the kitchen to visit with us. Right away she zeroed in on me, and with the biggest smile, she started teasing and patronizing me. To me she was the original Aunt Jemima incarnate — quite fat, jolly, great smile, wearing a white apron with some food stains. She introduced herself as Maude.

Maude went on to tell us she owned four restaurants in the area. She said her food was the best and asked what I wanted to order. I couldn't think of what to order, so she said, "How 'bout my favorite dish? Our famous hot beef sandwich smothered in gravy?"

I'd never had one, so I said, "Sure."

Maude asked me whether I played sports, and I said baseball, and Yogi Berra was my favorite player. She laughed and said, "Billy, I know you're good at it, but we need to put some meat on your bones." Mom, Dad, and brothers Jon and Bob were amused.

My first hot beef sandwich of my life was heavenly. Maude said, "I knew it. You just listen to Maude, Billy."

After the meal, we started to leave, and Maude came to the front door in her jolly way to give only me a hug. She said, "You must come again. Maude's is your kind of place."

The next day we hit a couple more historical sites in and around Appomattox and then headed north. When I couldn't stand it any longer, I blurted, "Dad, let's turn around and eat at Maude's."

He shook his head and said, "We have a schedule to keep."

I begged and begged, and finally the family voted three to two to turn around and head for Maude's and her scrumptious hot beef sandwich with lotsa gravy.

Maude spotted us in front, gathered me up in her arms, and pressed me against her big bosom. "I knew you'd come back for my hot beef sandwich, Billy." She made me feel so special. I'll never forget a minute of it.

I think we all wondered why she took a shine to me — a skinny, geeky looking boy from way up north with glasses and a big wave in his hair. But she did. She sure did, and I loved it so very much. I'll never forget Maude. So often I've hoped to meet someone from that part of Virginia so I could get information about Maude and her Hot Shops.

OL' JAY OF SAND LAKE

When I was eleven, I finally met a real Indian — an Ojibwa, named Jay. My friend Ron Erlandson took me to Jay's little log cabin in a small patch of woods near Sand Lake, Wisconsin. Back then I was caught up in the noble ethos of American Indians. I rooted for them in the cowboy and Indian movies. It intrigued me that the handicrafts and outdoor skills taught in Cub and Boy Scouts were taken from Indian lore. When I tramped in the woods, I pretended that I was an Indian scout. All the paths down by the Eau Claire River near my home were, in my mind, originally Ojibwa trails.

Ron and I walked one mile down a dusty gravel road from his cabin to the cut off path leading to Jay's cabin. The quarter mile path was bordered with clover and shrouded in spruce and poplar trees. The last thirty yards of the path were swampy, lined with bulrushes, a few cattails, and dank logs lying lengthwise to walk on giving off a soft springy sensation. His cabin was on higher ground nestled among sumac and conifer trees and shaded by Norway pine. There was a balsamic piney fragrance in the air. I couldn't wait!

When I saw him at the door, I greeted him with, "Hi Jay," and he muttered, "Lo."

At first sight, Jay reminded me of the stereotypical Hollywood Indian portrayed in cowboy movies. He wore a high top broad brimmed black hat with a colorful hatband. Jay was rawboned and skinny as a rail, and I was disappointed to notice that instead of moccasins he wore brown leather slippers that had stretchy elastic material in the middle. These slippers were popular in the forties and fifties. I called them grandpa slippers. He was wearing a white dress shirt, overalls, and black vest from a man's business suit.

To me Jay looked to be about 65 years old, but Ron thought he was close to 40. Being Ojibwa, Jay had the usual high cheekbones, and his face was thin with a hooked, narrow nostrils, and very thin lips. His eyes were deep brown and moist. Jay's cheeks and temples were hollow, and his hair was long, straight and stiff, like it was dirty. His skin was so brown it was almost black — smooth, shiny and seemed stretched as tight as a drum over his cheekbones and chin. I felt if I just touched his skin on the cheekbone with a sharp blade, it would split wide open across his entire face.

I asked Jay, "How's fishing?"

He responded, "I don't hunt or fish." He looked at Ron with a slight smile, and said, "Mother did all the hunting and fishing in our family, and I never learnt. She's dead now."

Ron asked, "What's your dad been up to?"

Jay gave Ron a knowing smile and said, "Going to Chippewa Falls to gamble I s'pose."

I welcomed a sudden cloudburst that forced us into his cabin giving me a chance to look around. Immediately I was struck by the strong smell from the kerosene lamps. There was a pot-bellied wood stove for heat and a wood-burning cook stove. The place was plain, and I noticed on the wall a dream catcher and a black and white photo of what I assumed were his parents. I craned my neck looking for more signs of Indian life. Had I seen buckskin moccasins or a shirt with any amount of beads on them, I would have been thrilled.

After the short rain, we went outside where there was a tree stump for chopping wood, a rusty axe, and several stacks of wood for the two stoves. There was also a garbage barrel filled with empty bottles and cans. It appeared Jay was kept alive by Old Crow whiskey and Dinty Moore beef stew.

None of us had more to say, so Ron and I said good-bye and started to mosey back to Ron's cabin. I said to Ron, "Well at least I met an actual Indian, but Ron, he didn't seem all that Indian to me. I will admit I could see some distant hint of Indian pride in him, but no spunk. He doesn't guide for hunting and fishing, doesn't even do it for the fun of it or for food, lives in a log cabin that looks like the kind early white settlers lived in, and he wears white man's clothing."

Ron smiled and stated, "His mother was the best fishing and hunting guide in the Sand Lake area." Ron added, "Jay's dad is really something. He wears a full red-beaded vest, a black derby hat with a feather, and he goes to Chippewa to an illegal gaming table when he gets his hands on extra money."

I asked Ron how Jay gets by, and he explained, "Jay does odd jobs for the summer cabin people, like helping them put in and take out docks and boats. All the Sand Lake people love him. He is so nice and willing to do favors for people, and he is good to the kids."

"Can Jay even build a campfire in the woods, Ron?"

Ron smiled and said, "Oh yah, he sure can. One time after he helped me put in our dock, we went fishing and I caught a northern pike. Jay suggested we eat it. We pulled into the island, he gathered wood for the fire, and I got a fry pan out of the boat. I thought it would be neat to see a real Indian build a fire in the woods. After collecting the branches, he went to his knapsack and took out a jar of kerosene and poured it all over the wood and struck a match. Man, did that sucker burn." That didn't seem Indian to me.

"Oh Ron, what's his last name?" I queried.

"Gee, I don't know. Nobody seems to know. I guess he doesn't have a last name." I was hoping he might have a last name like Black Bear or Eagle-something Indian. What the heck. I really didn't care what he was really like now. I'm going to tell the guys back home that I know a real north-country Indian.

ONE MORE PICKLE WILLY!

A literary sage once said, "Poems are maps to who we are." These lines from Kathy Mangan's poem, "Making Applesauce", bring back memories deeply imprinted in my heart and mind when I canned on hot August days with Aunt Mae and Mom.

> I bend my head over the pot,
> letting the sweet steam swirl
> into my eyes. The tears come,
> and while I stand here crying
> for you in my kitchen, your hands
> go on stirring, go on
> dignifying such simple acts.

To quote my friend Tommy Haugh, "It's the poets that bite the apple to the core."

For me it seems that some of the most mundane simple acts are the most endearing. Canning was a big deal in our house, and we three laid up canned goods in our cellar. It wasn't so much that I was requested to participate; it was more my being sequestered.

Mother announced, "Willy, tomorrow we can! So first we head to the supermarket to get the pears and peaches." The cucumbers and tomatoes were already in our backyard garden.

I loved the beautiful stickers on the wooden fruit crates we loaded into the car with scenes of orchards with names like San Fernando Pride, Golden Colorado, or Georgia Peaches Ya All, (showing a voluptuous wholesome girl with cheeks matching the hue of the peach she was eating). The scenes had a soothing, homely appeal.

Early in the morning of the day of our great enterprise, Mae and Mom got out the Mason and Kerr jars, jar tops, and rubber ringed lids from the cellar. We washed them in the stationary tubs in the basement and then sterilized them in boiling water. Mother yelled up the stairs to me, "Willy, get down here. We need you to start scrubbing the cucumbers." Ma was in charge — no ifs, ands, or buts about it.

Mae and Mom wore their oldest clothes. Mother had on a very plain looking sleeveless blouse and pedal pushers, and Mae was in an old fashion looking loose fitting cotton print sun dress. I had a feeling these were designated canning outfits and that I'd see them again next year at this time. The steam from the boiling water made their hair stringy, curled, and draped over their foreheads.

Dad, the accountant, liked the idea of canning. He did the math, and said, "All these savings will help come college tuition time." He liked trying to outfox the grocery stores high prices. This was why we raised our own chickens in our backyard in the middle of the city.

After I scrubbed the cucumbers with a stiff brush, Mother gave Mae and I new assignments. "Willy, your job will be to put pickles in the jars." Oddly, she didn't use the word cucumber; she referred to them as pickles even before the cucumbers were pickled.

Mae would hand me the pickle jar with sprigs of dill, vinegar, and garlic. I would shove the right sized cucs in the jar. I held the first jar up for all to admire, and Mother shook her head and said, "It's not full. One more pickle Willy! I want to hear them squeak when you shove them in."

I looked at Mae, and she rolled her eyes and told Mother, "For Pete's sake Irene. It looks full enough."

94

Ma would say, "I don't care. I know when a jar is full, and that one isn't. Another pickle Willy. You really have to pack them in. The pickles will get over it and find their peace." I always got another pickle in the jar. After we did umpteen jars of pickles, we switched to pears or peaches.

The fruits of our labor were beautiful on the cellar shelves. Glowing reds, yellows, and greens. Just to look at them gave me a sense of security, and I took comfort in knowing we'd always have plenty on hand.

Every spring while pickling ramps, I feel Aunt Mae and Mom's presence and Mangan's poem.

"Making Applesauce" from <u>Above the Tree Line</u> (1995) by Kathy Mangan reprinted with permission of Carnegie Mellon University Press.

OTTER CREEK

Rollie said, "My Dad used to catch nice brook trout in Otter Crick," as Hermie, Yogi, Butch, and Rollie jumped off their bikes at the Otter Creek Bridge.

Yogi blurted out, "Who's ever heard of anybody catching brook trout in this creek? It's full of quicksand, mud, and only has carp, suckers, chubs, and maybe one dumb catfish. It probably has more golf balls than trout."

Rollie said, "I heard at the Rod and Gun Club sporting goods store that the big deep pools still have some trout. Anyway, I got this steel telescopic rod and worm box for my birthday, and I want to try them. I dug some worms from the garden this morning."

After stashing their bikes in the bushes, the boys worked up a sweat trudging upstream from the bridge through the thick tag alders. Butch says with his lisp, "Them twouts are real smart, aren't they?"

Yogi says, "Yes they are too smart to live in Otter Creek."

Reaching the big pool below the back nine at the Eau Claire Country Club, Rollie rigged up his new rod and reached into the worm box on his belt and grabbed a worm. Rollie took several casts, and the line just floated slowly through the deep emerald colored pool without one twitch on the line. Time after time he cast to several parts of the big pool with no luck.

Yogi suggested that he forget it because he thought something as wild as a brook trout wouldn't live there. Butch restated, "Them twouts are too smart, right, Yog?"

All of a sudden there was a clatter behind a bush. They looked up, and it was Goopy on a boy's bike. Rollie asked, "Goopy, what are you doing here?"

She said, "Ann Bluedorn and I came here for a picnic. She left after we ate our sandwiches because it's so hot. I was going home the long way along this golfer's path hoping I'm not seen by any golfers."

Rollie turned to the other boys and said, "So hoorah, Goopy's here with all her red hair and freckles."

Goopy inquired, "What are you fishing for?"

"Twouts," said Butch.

Goopy says, "My dad and brothers fish brook trout near my uncle's farm in Lousy Creek, and last weekend they took me. We caught tons."

Rollie said, "Yah, just because you're a big tom-boy we're supposed to believe you can catch brook trout?"

Goopy replied, "I didn't know there were trout in Otter Creek."

Yogi replied, "We don't think so either, because we can't catch anything."

Goopy said "You need to fish where there is a cold spring coming into the creek. That's what we did last weekend."

Somebody said, "OK smarty pants, where is a cold spring?"

Goopy reached down into the creek with her hand, looked up and said, "This is really, really cold. There must be springs coming in somewhere."

Butch spoke up, "Well I guess them twouts are frozen down there because they don't eat our worms."

Goopy piped up, "Last weekend we caught them on grasshoppers. That's the best thing to use in August, according to my dad."

Rollie suggested, "Your bike is saying take me home, Goop! Isn't it time for you to leave? Don't you know that gray clouds in the sky means rain is coming? I've never heard of using grasshoppers."

Goopy said, "We caught them last weekend on live grasshoppers. I'll look for some."

Rollie muttered, "Go ahead Goop, but I think we're going home."

Goopy asks Butch for his cap to put grasshoppers in.

Butch says, "Heck no. I don't want any icky grasshoppers in my cap. Use your paper lunch bag." Goopy trudged through deep sand to a grassy area to search for the hoppers.

Yogi asked Goop, "What's that song you're humming?"

Goopy replied, "'I Love Those Dear Hearts and Gentle People Who Live in My Home Town'. It's my favorite."

As Goopy walked off, Rollie turned to the other guys and said, "You know everything she wears is a hand me down. Did you notice that her socks are bunched up in the middle of her feet? That's because they're too small and slip off her heels."

Yogi added, "Those Irish families have hundreds of kids, so they share their clothes."

Rollie yelled at Goop, "Hey Goop, I suppose you Catholics will be going to Sacred Heart Junior High School in the seventh grade to be taught by nuns. Is it true they have holy water in the drinking fountains at Sacred Heart?"

"Yup, that's true," said Goop. "And at St. Patrick's High School, we're called the Fighting Irish. Our symbol is the shamrock, and our colors are green and white. Isn't that nice?"

Goopy walked through the tall grass, and grasshoppers of all colors and sizes burst into flight clicking and snapping. Some just hung on the slender grasses where she very carefully cupped her gentle hands and softly lifted them off the swaying tall grasses. She gathered about a dozen hoppers, shoved them in the sack and returned to the group. The guys looked bored and defeated.

Butch asked, "Them bugs catch fish, huh?"

Goopy stated, "Sure do. Let me show you how you put them on the hook." The guys were all eyes when they saw the hoppers antennas waving in the breeze, and when she handed a hopper to Rollie the hopper spit tobacco juice on his finger.

Rollie dropped it and exclaimed, "Hell no."

Goopy grabbed a big brown grasshopper and said, "Here, I'll do it."

Rollie told Goop that he knew Catholics go to confession once a week, but he'd heard that she had to go three times a week. The boys giggled.

Goopy said, "Really, my priest wants me to go every day." The boys giggle again.

"Just what we thought," said Rollie.

"OK," says Goop, "I'll show you how to do this. First, this hook is too big. Do you have a small, thinner hook?" Rollie found one in his little tin box and handed it to Goopy. She suggested, "This will do, but I'll have to take the sinker off the line. You don't want the weight of the sinker to pull the hopper under water and drown it. This clear cat gut line is OK too." She removed the sinker, tied on the hook, and used her teeth to bite off the excess line dangling from the knot. "You hook the hopper through the back of the neck. That's what my dad does, and the hopper stays alive. You want the hopper to wiggle and kick on top of the water."

Yogi was rather tickled by the way she removed the sinker, changed the hook on the line, and slipped the hook through the grasshopper. She was so earnest and sure of what she was doing, yet feminine and eloquent about it. Her fingers were pretty, nimble, slim, and delicate. He had never noticed a girl's fingers up close before, but he wondered what it would be like to touch, feel, and hold her fingers and hands. All the boys were gathered around her with their heads down watching in great anticipation. Yogi thought she looked kind of nice with her newly tanned arms and sunburned peeling nose. After the hopper was attached to the hook, she looked up at Yogi and with the cutest smile she said, "What do you think of that Yogi?"

"Oh neat, really neat," was his response.

Butch said, "That's nifty Goopy."

She said, "There Rollie. Go catch a trout," as she walked down to the creek.

All three boys looked at Yogi, and Rollie said, "What do you think of that Yogi?"

The other three boys said in unison, "What do you think of that Yogi?" The three laughed and Rollie says, "I think you and Goopy like each other. Yogi has a crush on Goopy of all people, ha ha."

Yogi blushed a little and told them, "You drips can drop dead."

Rollie said, "You can't just slough it off Yog."

Butch suggested, "Yogi, go pick a bouquet for your new girlfriend, and the rest of us will go catch a twout." Yogi followed the guys to the stream.

Everybody stood along the stream bank and watched as Rollie cast the line into an alder bush. Butch rolled his eyes and put his hands on his hips. Butch and Yogi scampered over and untangled the line so Rollie could cast again. This time the line landed on the water, and the hopper floated on the edge of the creek as it bounced and twisted around some watercress just under the tag alders with no bite.

Goopy yells, "Wait I'll go up by that stump and throw a couple hoppers in the water to see if they excite any trout to eat them." She walked twenty yards on a high knoll above the pool and tossed a couple of the hoppers into the water. Everybody watched intently as the critters kicked toward shore. There was a sudden breeze causing a riffle across the water and with all the sunshine, reflections off the bushes and the multicolor hues of the stream, the boys lost track of the hoppers and couldn't see them at all. All of a sudden, a gulp and a pink flash in the water and one of the hoppers was gone.

Goopy saw it all from her vantage point and screamed. "Holy cow, that was a brook trout. Did you see that? Rollie get that line in the water again, fast!"

Rollie cast the line in the water, and it drifted and bobbed around some overhanging grass with no strike. "Toss it in the middle of the pool," yelled Goop. Rollie cast again and, it landed all tangled up in a willow tree near the bank of the creek.

"Dagnammit," said Rollie.

Butch told him, "Pull like hell Wollie. It might unhook." The line released and on the next cast he landed the hopper in the middle of the big emerald pool. The hopper drifted three feet kicking like crazy toward shore when all of a sudden a *WHOOOSH*, and the water exploded. A great fish rocketed out of the water. It must have jumped a foot into the air, and it landed on the water with a splash that sent a wake into the shore.

"Holy mackerel," yelled Rollie, and he just stood there stunned.

Goopy yelled, "Holy cow!" and just plopped down on her seat with her skinny white legs dangling over the edge of the eroded creek bank as she almost slipped off into the rocks ten feet below.

Butch shouted, "Cheezus Cwise," and put both hands on this head.

Hermie said, "It's a monster."

Yogi said, "I think it's a big brook trout — an eighteen or twenty incher."

Rollie's reel started screaming as it peeled off-line. The trout took another somersaulting jump. Then the trout headed upstream, licka-de-split, as the line made a V in the water.

Goopy advised, "Don't let the line get caught on that stump." Sure enough, the line did get caught on the stump. Goop scrambled down the bank and waded into the shallow riffle above the snag to try releasing the line. She eventually got the line free, and the trout retreated to the middle of the big pool. All of them could see the flashing muted colors of the trout under the surface as it struggled against the line. After a few more seconds of thrashing, the big trout was on the surface nearly spent. Rollie pulled the trout in toward himself and reached down to grab the fish. The trout was so big and slippery that it slipped and did a pirouette in the air and then torpedoed to the bottom of the deep pool.

The fish was still hooked, and Goopy suggested, "It's too slippery to grab. Just pull it onto the shore."

Rollie took that suggestion, and as he held the rod, he walked backward slowly pulling it onto the sandbar, and he just fell on the fish. Everybody ran over to the sandbar to admire the fish, and Hermie proclaimed that it was a world record brook trout. Goopy suggested cutting a V shaped branch to hang the giant trout on. Yogi used his jackknife to cut the branch, and Rollie raised the fish.

"Wow," said Goopy.

"Wow," said Rollie and Yogi.

Hermie asked, "Are you going to mount it?" Butch suggested eating it.

Rollie said, "I don't know yet, but I'm showing it to everybody."

"Let's bring it to the Rod and Gun Club sports shop and display it in the glassed-in ice box in front of the store," said Yogi.

The whole gang headed home with Rollie steering his bike with one hand and holding the branch with the fish in the other. Hermie carried Rollie's rod as he biked. At the corner of Sherwin and Emery streets, Hermie turned to Goopy and said, "We're going over to Rollie's house, see ya."

She answered, "Oh ya, I guess I'll head home."

Butch asks Goop, "Just how did you get the name Goopy anyway?"

Goopy pretended not to hear him.

At Rollie's house, they cleaned the fish off with the garden hose and stood admiring the shimmering trout. The trout had a bluish green back with yellow squiggly markings. The sides of the trout were greenish yellow with blue spots that had maroon spots in the center. The fins were scarlet red with bright white edges. They marveled at the beauty of the fish and congratulated each other on their great feat. Finally, they all agree that Rollie was a champion fisherman who seemed impossible to beat. Rollie suggested that they go again tomorrow saying, "Heck we're the experts. We know how to catch them."

PALMER METHOD

One of the things Mother drummed into our heads was to send thank you notes to all who gave us Christmas and birthday gifts — a gift at any time actually.

I remember in the 1940's the Eau Claire School Board sent a person to each grade school every year to teach the Palmer Method of cursive writing. Some referred to it as longhand writing. These lessons started in the 2nd grade with pencils and lined pages. By the fourth grade, we advanced into dip pens in ink.

The sessions were fine with me because it was a nice diversion from numbers, spelling, and reading. Maybe deep down inside I felt it was sort of like drawing — touching on art. Our instructor explained that cursive means, ". . .letters joined together with a flowing appearance." He stated it was started in 1888 and was now the fastest growing, most popular handwriting-style. Faster than the previous Spencerian Script in the U.S.A.

Standing by the blackboard, he started by telling us the importance of written correspondence. Then he sat at a desk and demonstrated the big role posture plays in good writing. All new to us! We were ready to be launched into this new world.

I think I remember that not all, but some of our desks had ink wells. So, in fourth grade our instructor showed us how to load ink into our pen holders without spilling our precious ink. Our pens had metal nibs. And the big surprise to me was that none of us made a mess with ink.

On the blackboard, our lettering instructor scripted the whole alphabet in upper and lower case letters. Then, he did each and every letter in slow motion for us to observe.

He emphasized that we be brave. So, we started, and right away it was obvious most of us were too timid, making *ohhh* such small letters. He admonished, "Do bold strokes. Show off a little with bigger loops on top and bottom. And whatever you do, try your hardest to make your letters connect gracefully like I demonstrated on the blackboard." He added, "The upper loops are ascenders and the lower are descenders, but those are big words. I don't expect you to learn all those terms today." He added, "With your teacher, you'll practice lettering a little every day till the school year ends."

Our instructor expressed that personal letters, well done, are a social grace and a nicely addressed envelope shows respect for the person you're sending to. "You might as well know that you will be writing like this the rest of your life, so you'd better start learning it now." This sounded like lofty stuff to me, and I noticed that Rollie Jacobs slowly shook his head a little, and Herman Manthie rolled his eyes.

When Mother was pretty old, she handed me a letter I sent to my cousins when I was ten years old. She said Aunt Grace saved it to give to us someday. What a kick! I sent a copy to cousins Charles and Jim, and they loved it. The letter is in Palmer cursive, and I added a couple drawings. At my Second Ward grade school we once had an Indian chief from Black River Falls, WI. demonstrate his bird calls. His name was Chief Evergreen Tree and he looked stunning in white buckskin with the most gorgeous head dress of beads and eagle feathers. I was so enamored with him that one of the drawings on the letter to my cousins is of him. Seems I was compelled way back then to add a flourish.

I've never stopped sending scripted notes and letters in Palmer as well as other cursive hands. People like the personal touch, and they rarely fail to express their appreciation.

Now I'm a member of a calligraphy guild, and that has added to my passion of keeping hand-written lettering alive in this technology age.

Elegy for the Personal Letter by Allison Joseph

I miss the rumpled corners of correspondence,
the ink blots and cross-outs, that show
someone lives on the other end, a person
whose hands make errors, leaves traces.
I miss fine stationary, its raised elegant
lettering prominent on creamy shades of ivory
or pearl grey. I even miss hasty notes
dashed off on notebook paper, edges
ragged as their scribbled messages-
can't much write now-thinking of you.
When letters come now, they are formatted
by distant computer, addressed
to Occupant or To the family living at-
meager greetings at best,
salutations made by committee.
Among the glossy catalogs
and one time only offers
the bills and invoices,
letters arrive so rarely now that I drop
all other mail to the floor when
an envelope arrives and the handwriting
Is actual handwriting, the return address
somewhere I can locate on any map.
So seldom is it that letters come
that I stop everything else
to identify the scrawl that has come this far-
the twist and whirl of the letters,
the loops and the numerals. I open those
envelopes first, forgetting that
chain of any other mail,
hoping for news I could not read
in any other way but this.

Published with permission from the author Allison Joseph.

REMEMBERING BENNY

For the last year, I've been watching the obituaries in the Minneapolis Star Tribune for an announcement of my first friend Tommy Benson's death. Finally, on April 17 it appeared, but to my surprise his death was declared unexpected. I knew Tom had life threatening health problems including cirrhosis of the liver. Tom was on the list for a liver transplant. But, dying unexpectedly, that sounded like an accident.

The first funeral service was at Gainey Ranch in Scottsdale, Arizona. Five days later the family had a service at Werness Bros. Funeral Home in southwest Minneapolis for the Minnesota and Wisconsin crowd. At the Minneapolis service, I learned that because of Tommy's health problems he passed out on the Gainey Ranch golf course and hit his head on a bench, which resulted in his death. For anybody else, the blow to the head would have left a black and blue mark and maybe a headache. But, Tommy was a bleeder, and his head filled with blood. They tried to drain the blood at the hospital with no success; he expired. Somebody said it was a good thing he died because, had he lived, he would have been so screwed up it would have been a pity. The obituary stated, "Tom died doing what he loved, golfing."

At the age of 66 Tom left behind his wife Mary Lou, eight children, fourteen grandchildren, and two great grandchildren.

Tom was my first grade school friend at Second Ward Grade School. One Friday in spring of first grade we walked home together. The next day I rode my trike to his house to play all morning. To our surprise we both wore Junior Commando sweatshirts our mothers got us from the Farmers Store. At noon Tom's mother served us Campbell's tomato soup, hotdog, a chocolate chip cookie, and Kool Aid. I thought it was a royal feast because it was the first time I felt like a real guest. Tom and I became fast friends from that day on. I still remember his phone number seventy-five years later, 5096.

Tom and I were small but fast. We played half back on the football team and guards in basketball. We both felt good when the other ran interference for the other in football. In the summer at Boyd Park, Tommy was the pitcher, and I was the catcher on the baseball team. My all time favorite childhood memories are of playing baseball with Tommy in the citywide summer league.

One big grade school memory was in sixth grade when I got jealous of all the attention Tom was getting when demonstrating a spinning top on a string to our classmates, mostly girls. I was jealous of the attention he was getting so I hit the string and the whirling top crashed to the floor. Tom glared up at me when he picked up the top and said, "We'll meet in the playground after school to settle this."

Not thinking of a believable excuse to get out of a fight, I had a queasy stomach the rest of the day. I thought, how dumb. How did I get myself in this jam with my best friend? I felt he was tougher than me, and he'd probably beat the hell out of me and embarrass me in front of all those schoolmates.

There was a good crowd gathered in the playground when we met. We started pushing each other, then fists flew. To my surprise I held my own, but to be honest neither of us tried very hard. Not many minutes later a teacher came along to break up the fight. I was relieved. When my mother got home after school, I caught holy hell. She said, "I subbed today at Second Ward and at the end of the day I looked out the window to see my own son in a fight." She said she was so mad because she attended Eau Claire State Teachers College with a couple of the teachers and Principal Stokes, and now I had embarrassed her.

The next day Tom and I arrived at school wearing our Cub Scout shirts. Thursday was designated scout day at our school. It seemed odd to me that we were friendly with each other, and our anger was all gone. Tom and I talked it over and decided that real Cub Scouts don't settle things by fighting. We had pledged that at one of our pack #17 club meetings. Dad said, "You guys got it off your chests." I knew in my heart that I liked, Tom, and I was glad it was over and ended happily.

Another special memory for me was in the seventh grade. By then Tom had enrolled in Sacred Heart Junior High School, and I was in Eau Claire Junior High School. Tom called me on a Sunday and said, "How about going to the St. Patrick's High School football game this afternoon?"

I said, "No, I'm out of money already except one thin dime."

Tommy said, "No sweat the game only costs ten cents." I couldn't believe it. The Eau Claire H.S. games on Friday nights were twenty-five cents.

So, with a borrowed bus token from brother Bob, Tom and I went to the St. Pat's and La Crosse Cathedral H.S. football game. Even back then I knew this was the best deal in town.

At the game while milling around, I was surprised how Tom acted toward the priests and Catholic brothers. Tom seemed real relaxed and comfortable in this Catholic setting. Kind of like he found his place after leaving public school. Tom always addressed those in black as Father. It was, "Yes Father, or thank you Father, and I certainly will, Father." There were plenty of nuns, but Tom seemed to steer clear of them. This was the first time for me, being surrounded by so many Catholics and it gave me a curious feeling. But soon I felt comfortable, even though this crowd knew I wasn't Catholic because I didn't address the clergy with, yes Father and certainly brother.

My family moved from Eau Claire to Minneapolis after eighth grade. My parents continued to receive the Eau Claire Telegram newspaper, so I occasionally heard about Tom's athletic career at Regis, the new Catholic high school. Tom was a real star in three sports. He set a conference record for his long punts.

When I met with Tom several years later, he said the Reverend Father Paul helped him build character during his high school years. I remembered Father Paul. He was the most handsome man in Eau Claire. My mother said all the catholic girls were mad when he took the church for his bride instead of one of them. Tom said, "Father Paul said I was my own worst enemy because I was too hard on myself." Father Paul would say, "It's not your fault when we lose just because you are the quarterback." He helped Tom keep things in perspective.

Tom was a real star athlete at Regis, and his girlfriend, Mary Lou, was a total doll. As a couple, they were stars. After high school, Tom and Mary Lou got married. By the time I got out of college, Tommy and Mary Lou had four kids.

Tom had the city desk job at National Presto, so he knew the product line. The company sent Tom to a trade show at Chicago's Merchandise Mart to explain their home appliance products to manufacturers' representatives and distributors. The reps were so impressed with Tom that he got a job offer from the Edelston Company of Chicago. Tom took the leap and joined Edelston. The Edelston Co. sent Tom and family to Minneapolis to represent their line of products on straight commission. This was right up Tom's alley. A job where there was no limit to what he could earn in sales commissions. Tom had no desire for a safer sales job that provided a salary, company car, paid expenses, and insurance benefits. Tom knew there was a ceiling to his earnings in that scenario. Tom had the guts, brains, and enough greed to seize the big opportunity of sky's the limit straight commission. He had a big nut to crack. Tom was the best in his field, a real high roller, retiring very wealthy in his early sixties to become a golf nut in Arizona.

At the funeral, Tom's business partner gave a touching and funny talk about their special relationship. Tom's repping partner called him Benny, a name I gave Tommy in the sixth grade. I was happy to hear the name stuck. In his talk he cited examples of how at Target Corporation buyers row, the purchasing agents would see Benny coming down the aisle and they would yell things like, "Hey, Benny, add twenty more gross to that toaster order, and while you're at it, let's get that sixty gross of cappuccino brewers we talked about," or, "Benny, can you get me this or that?" Or, "Benny I have a manufacturer who is looking for a good representative, do you want me to get you the line?" This was how highly regarded Benny was to these buyers.

Goopy and her husband drove in from Madison for the funeral, and we sat together. She, Tom, and I were oldest grade school friends. I was doing all right during the funeral until they played "Danny Boy". Not fair! How do you keep a dry eye at an Irish funeral when they play "Danny Boy"? To me the Irish have the most beautifully sentimental songs.

After "Danny Boy" and "When Irish Eyes are Smiling", the people started to file out carrying their programs with the Irish prayer, "May the road rise to meet you. May the wind be always at your back. . .". I went up front to the open casket to see Benny. He was wearing his Gainey Ranch golf wind- breaker and at his side a framed score card of his best round of golf. I told him, "You did it Benny. You showed them all. Talk about guts. Benny, it seemed the cards were stacked against you, but you used that predicament to motivate yourself, and you rose above it to become a huge success in every way." I admit I felt small standing there, feeling he was superior to me. How would I have fared with those same challenges?

I told him, "It was tough losing my first friend. You know, Benny, nobody ran the ball and interference better than you. Remember when we'd go the Boyd Park for tackle football? None of us had more than one piece of padding. Either we had a helmet or shoulder pads and we shared them with our brothers. If someone showed up with both, we'd feel it almost unfair. You ran and kicked the ball well and I specialized in end runs and shoestring tackles.

I wanted to see you again to tell you that I finally tracked down Goopy after 55 years, and that she and I were planning a Boyd Park reunion. It won't be the same without you. I was also hoping to get you down to Eau Claire for the YMCA golf event to raise money for Y youth programs. The fundraiser is in memory of Clayton Anderson and the event raises approximately 40K. Remember, Benny, how we went to the Y every Saturday in winter?"

I told him, "The Priest and your sales repping partner made reference to Bunny's Tavern as your watering hole. Had I known that, I would have stopped at Bunny's to bend an elbow with you from time to time." Finally, I said, "Good-bye old friend and thanks for everything. You did it well, you loved everybody and showed immense humanity in the way you conducted your life." Finally, I added, "Jesus, had you lived to 85, you probably would have been a great, great grandfather. How many of them do we know?"

SAND LAKE

Life was good for me on the east side hill, but the real special treats were visiting my cousins dairy farm near Cornell and being invited to Erlandson's Sand Lake cabin. Sand Lake was up Highway 40, north of Bloomer, and just south of Island Lake. We charged up #40 passing cars, clicking on the dimmer switch on the floorboard from dim to bright, and reading several Burma Shave signs as the car radio faded out when we got out of range of local radio stations.

My fishing buddy Ron Erlandson knew how to get me overly excited when he'd spin yarns about how the biggest northern pike were on the rampage in their lake and how we'd catch them like mad this month of September. I was swooning. I could hardly sleep the night before we left for their cabin.

Sand Lake was only about forty miles north of Eau Claire, but it seemed to be in a different zone. In the morning, the lake had fog on the surface, and there was a chill in the air. This was the first time I learned of a bird called the loon and heard its iconic song. What a thrill. Storms had more gusto than in the city. Yup, we were up north, and I could hardly contain myself.

There were so many new discoveries. One was diving off the dock and coming up with clams. We'd open the clam shells and cut out the orange meaty part to use for bait. The bluegills would rise up and gobble it just as it hit the water. All new to a worm dunker like me.

Ron taught me how they put a perch or small sunfish on a big hook and cast it out as far as possible. Then he stuck the pole between two slats at end of the dock. We all sat on chairs near the dock and watched for the bobber to disappear. Ron would run to the pole and haul the northern pike in and place it in the live box.

That first night, take-charge Ron announced that tomorrow we'd get up at four AM and go fishing northern pike. He looked but couldn't find the alarm clock, so he said he'd put some wood in the stove. He claimed by four, the fire would go out and the cabin would chill down and that would wake us. I had my doubts, but for crying out loud, it worked. How clever of Ron.

This was my first time in a boat with an outboard motor. We used Eppinger red and white daredevil spoon lures and a floating lure called an injured minnow. I'd jerk the injured minnow lure so it looked crippled, and the northerns slammed it. This was my first time catching northerns. I caught three, but no monsters.

Ron didn't want to bring too many fish back to the cabin, so he released some which almost gave me a conniption. He said his parents didn't want to load up the live box.

It wasn't long until I was hungry and looked for lunch. Julia, Ron's mother, said they would eat around 12:30, and it was only 9:00! I was amazed because it seemed like I had been up for so long already. Ron's mom staked out a couple northerns, and they were delicious. I never knew northerns were so good.

113

After supper, all of us went to McGills Resort and hung out in the tavern while Ron's parents nursed about three Walters beers each. This was my first exposure to the mysterious world of a tavern. I wondered how I'd keep it a secret from Mom and Dad that I was in a tavern until midnight.

Ron and I mostly played the jukebox and chatted with a guy who said there was a musky in the lake known as Jingle Bell. This guy claimed the fish had been hooked and broken the line so many times that the lures were still in its lips. When the musky jumped while hooked and shook its head, it sounded like jingle bells. Wanting to believe it was true, I bought the story hook, line, and sinker. In the end, he smiled and confessed he was only spoofing us.

The colorful Wurlitzer jukebox was great. It took almost all my lawn mowing earnings. One song the patrons played over and over again was the popular "Tennessee Waltz", sung by Patti Page. Ron and I played mostly hillbilly laments including Hank Williams, of course. I got a kick out of the restrooms with names "Bucks" and "Does".

When World War II ended, the US government offered returning vets quanset huts to transition to. After the huts served their purpose, they were sold to the general public for approximately $300. These huts were bought to be placed on farms, industrial sites, and on lakeshores. Ron's dad, Hal bought one and with his friend disassembled the hut, cleaned it up, and the pieces were loaded into the truck and reassembled on Sand Lake. The Erlandson family dolled up the hut with flowers and shrubs along all four sides. They put in a brick walkway from the front door through the grass. Inside they made it so cozy. On the walls they had pictures of ducks from Seagram's calendars. Also, these scenes were on glass plates.

Three cabins down from Erlandson's was the Sneen's place. Edrian and Laura Sneen had their nieces from Elk Mound, WI. as guests. The Sneen's went to McGills for dinner, so Ron and I were with the girls. Ron knew them from previous visits to Sand Lake, so he felt familiar enough to suggest playing spin the bottle. That made me nervous thinking I might have to kiss a girl.

I'd played the game before with Rollie Jacobs, Gretchen Schmitt, and Ellie Olson one cold spring day on one of the greens at the Eau Claire

Country Club Golf Course. But at this event, we kissed the girls' hands, and they'd say, "I'll never wash this kiss off my hand for the rest of my life." A romantic notion that made us boys feel good.

Ron started the spinning and suddenly the empty milk bottle pointed at me, so it was my chance to kiss one of the girls. Of course, I chose the cutest little blond. Oh my God, my heart was racing as Ron smirked. I mustered the courage and hastily planted a kiss on this cutie and basically missed her lips by a half. So, it was a marginal kiss. I felt like such a dud. Screwing up my first kiss, I wondered what she must have thought. I felt a little guilty about kissing a girl. Was this rushing things or just another natural right of passage?

To this day whenever I hear Patti Page's lovely "Tennessee Waltz" it takes me back to Sand Lake and my first kiss. Really quite a nice memory.

SIMPLE GIFT

My cousin Charles and I were the same age and his brother Jim was a year younger. I loved going to their farm and Charles loved visiting me in the big city. Jim could take or leave my city.

Charles wasn't all that fond of farming. Rather, he was scholarly and urbane. Charles knew at a young age that he wanted to be a chemist.

Jim and I shared an interest in farm work and the great outdoors. We were the explorers, always tramping in the woods near his farm or by the river that flowed through my city. We pretended to be Indian scouts. Our plans were to farm together when we grew up. Jim was active in 4-H and every year he showed his calves at the Chippewa County Fair.

Myself, I was all outdoors. I was the sport, playing football in the fall, basketball in the winter and baseball in spring and summer. When not at the park playing sports, I was fishing the river.

I stayed in athletics and fishing. My cousins entered into scouting. After Cub Scouts they went on to reach the highest levels in Boy Scouting, earning the ultimate merit badges.

Much to my disappointment Dad never signed me up for Boy Scouts. Our scouting program in my city hit dire straits when the head of the Cub Scouts absconded with our annual carnival money, putting a damper on Boy

Scouting prospects. Also, I slipped through the cracks because we moved from Eau Claire to Minneapolis.

But one special visit to my cousins stands out in my mind. Ma delivered me to Cornell for a three-day visit. Instead of dropping me off at the farm, Mom and Aunt Grace dropped me at the Boy Scout gathering at Brunet State Park to meet up with Charles and Jim. When I got there, I was wide eyed with the sights and sounds of the camp. The scouts were all decked out in their uniforms. They were wearing shirts with their achievement patches, cool-looking blousy kerchiefs with crafty handmade neckerchief slides. Some slides were woodcarvings of forest animals like the bear or wolf, others were colorful Indian Chief head dresses. Many of the scouts even wore shorts and knee-high brown wool socks with garters. On the bottom of the garter was either a green or red strip, green for Boy Scout and red for Explorer Scout. Some of the kids wore special scout caps with a badge sewn on that showed their achievement level. The Scout Master wore a smart looking broad brimmed brown hat.

The pavilion where the scouts met enchanted me. The building was made of logs with fireplaces made from huge rocks. In the fireplaces were big fires that smelled, oh so good, and gave an orange glow to the whole scene. The flurry of activity invited me.

I walked into the gathering and was bowled over. The scouts were doing all the things I wanted to do! Learning to tie knots, (I'm a knots challenged person to this day), carve wood, plan service programs, learn animal tracking, and other nature related things. They were even planning their annual trip to Philmont in Cimarron, New Mexico, a national scout camp where they learned western skills like lassoing, horseback riding, mountaineering, mule pack tripping, trout fishing and climbing. This was where I belonged!

My cousins spotted me and said, "Great Bill, we'll put our stuff away and take you to the house." I said, "You can't be serious about leaving all this to spend the night with me back at your place." "Sure," they said, "Certainly, we can do this any old time. We want to be with you and hear all about what you have been doing." How could they leave this to be with little ol me, I wondered? At that point I figured the Boy Scouts had more character than the rest of us. This flabbergasted me. I had never experienced a time when I felt more special. This was their kindest <u>Simple Gift</u> to me.

When we went back to their farm that night, we simply played board games, and a few records and then we went to bed. The next morning, we took their pup tent and pitched it in their woods. We cooked hotdogs and roasted marshmallows and had a blast just exploring their fairly ordinary woods that we'd explored a zillion times.

When college started, my cousins and I started to drift apart, only seeing each other during usual holidays like Christmas. When Charles and I met, we often talked about subjects like photography. As for Jim, he was off somewhere pouring over his botany books. His plants in his botany lab became his mistress. Marriage for both of them came immediately after college graduation. They both went on to graduate school, Charles in chemistry and Jim in botany.

How time changes some of our most fundamental values. I take comfort in knowing that way back in the ninth grade I did receive a Simple Gift from both of them when they chose me over spending the night at that exotic scout camp. This I hold dear. I can't explain why such a little gesture like that has stayed with me, but I will never forget it. My cousins Charles and Jim made the "Where Friends and Nature Meet" sign above the fireplace in that glowing pavilion.

SPEED SKATING

The racers looked so sleek with flashing blades as they gracefully swooshed around the curves with their arms behind their backs. Speed skating was a glamour sport to me while growing up during the 1940's in Eau Claire.

In the sixth grade I decided to enter my first skating race. I figured because I was hard to catch but could catch others with ease in Pom Pom Pull Away, I was ready for racing. There was some talk of speed skating at our supper table and my older brother Bob asked for racer skates for Christmas. It seemed to me racing was a natural progression.

Dad read in the newspaper about a citywide junior speed skating event at Boyd Park so when he asked, I jumped at the chance. Two days before the race I brought my skates to Haugen's Shoe Repair for sharpening. That night I gave my skates a little ice time to take off the too sharp edge in order to get them in perfect condition for Saturdays race. Friday the rink was flooded in preparation for the next day races.

After a hardy breakfast, with an extra bowl of Cheerios, Dad walked me to Boyd Park. Several people milled around, and some older racers wore tights for less wind resistance. There were two men in charge, each wearing a badge and whistle, and one holding a pistol. It all seemed so official I started to get butterflies in my stomach. I even had second thoughts about plunging into this new sport. My skates were plain black general-purpose skates, not the long blade racer skates.

Dad and I found my group and my heart sank when I saw Lefty Rada. We all knew he was the best athlete my age in Eau Claire. Lefty looked rough and ready in his black and white checkered wool shirt and brown leather pilots cap and he had his usual resolute look on his face. I wore my brother's elk sweater, and I tucked my pants into my wool stockings, so I looked racy too.

The official announced our race was about fifteen to twenty minutes away and that we could take some warmup laps on the perimeter of the racing track. I took laps all right, way too many. I felt important out there because by now we already had numbers pinned on our backs, and I thought it real neat to be seen by Dad and some of my classmates as a racer warming up.

By the time the race started my legs were already tired. Five of us lined up, and the official pulled out his pistol and said, "Ready, set" and pop went the pistol. Off we go! I skated like crazy, looking straight ahead and telling myself not to fall. Halfway through the course my legs felt like rubber and became weak, but Lefty and I led the pack. At the very end of the race, just before the finish line my upper legs wore out and started spreading farther apart until I did the splits and a perfect belly flop sliding across the finish line, being edged out by Lefty. Looking around I thought, thank God my heart throb Julie Nelson wasn't here to see this. I could hardly get up with my legs so weak and wobbly. Dad ran up to me and in a half scolding way said, "You got second place, how come you fell"? I vowed never to warm up too much again.

Even though I fell, I was OK with finishing so close to Lefty. The official handed me the first speed skating medal of my life, so I thought I was a star. The second-place medal was about the size of a dime, and I thought it was stunning. Classmates, Maxine Brandt and Lois Jordan also won medals. Dad and I walked home, and I ran ahead to burst into the house and yelled, "I won a medal and it's a beauty." Mother was all excited and said, "Willy, you simply floated through the door on a cloud." At Mother's suggestion I sat down and wrote Aunt Mae in Chicago about winning a medal. Mae always wanted to hear about her nephew's achievements, and I wanted to please her the most so I'd be her favorite.

Because of that race I felt like a speed skater, so I was into a new fantasy. I begged my parents for tights and racer skates like the real hotshots wore, but my plea fell on deaf ears. With my Christmas money from Aunt Mae and a dollar loan from Dad I bought a pair of twelve-inch racer skates from a kid down the block. I was ready for another race.

The next speed skating event was across town at Kaiser Field. Right away somebody pointed at a kid and said, "That's Jack Grewe, he's really good and he's in sixth grade at Third Ward Grade School." Looking at Jack made me feel inadequate because Jack not only wore racer-skates, he had a sporty looking black nylon wind breaker with zippers. I knew the Third Ward was where the rich people lived and Jack looked really sharp, well contained, and way too calm. He seemed to know a lot of people, so I figured this was Jack's "home rink." That's when I noticed the red, blue, yellow and green lines marking the racers lanes. That made me feel this event was a big deal which added to my nervousness, but I figured after all I already had a medal and did well against Lefty and I don't see him here. All of a sudden here comes Lefty in his same plaid shirt and pilots cap huffing and puffing with his skates slung over his shoulder, and I felt faint of heart thinking about facing Grewe and Lefty.

The race director told us to warm up before the race and I vowed not to overdo it but with my nervous energy I took too many laps and feared I overdid it again. Dad said, "Pace yourself in this one, (I'd never heard of that before) by starting slow and saving energy for a strong spurt near the finish line."

Get ready, get set, pop — Jack and I busted out front of the pack with Jack getting a little ahead of me ,and I'm telling myself not to fall and to save some energy for the finish. I gritted my teeth and remembered doing the splits with Lefty at Boyd Park and vowed not to do that again and praying for the finish line to appear before my legs made me flop. Lefty went a little too wide on a curve and I got the edge on him. Amazingly enough I caught Grewe at the finish line in a tie with Lefty swooping in inches behind us. The director said there wasn't enough time (and the ice had ruts from all the races) for a run-off between us two winners. He asked if we'd agree to a flip of a coin to determine the winner and we said OK and I got the call. Dad whispered in my ear, "Call tails." But because after all I was the racer, and a little puffed up from tying with Jack, I showed my independence by calling heads. The coin landed tails up and the bright shiny medal the size of a quarter went to Jack. Dad was aghast at my insolence. On our way home he scolded me about how tails usually wins. I couldn't believe his ardent disgust with me losing out on the first-place medal. I wondered how he could be so sure it would be tails. It was only fifty, fifty chance I figured. Happily, the next week I got a silver and bronze duplicate first place medal in the mail. To this day I've always called tails, but I can't say it has furthered my fortunes in any way.

My speed skating days ended after the seventh grade because I decided to be a ski flyer on the Flying Eagles ski jumping team. Looking back, I am glad I had the speed skating experience because I thought racers were an elite group above social skaters. It also helped me to never fear starting a new sport. I won two medals in speed skating and an appreciation for graceful skaters with flashing blades. A few years later Bob gave me his eighteen inchers and after sixty some years they are in a box in the basement and once in a while I take them and go skating. I will never miss the World Olympic speed skating events on TV. I fantasize that I'm one of the racers.

SPRING FEVER

The smell of mothballs, rare these days, reminding me of our cedar chest, brings back fond memories of Henry's Sport Shop. The owner Orrin Stanwick, Henry's son, used mothballs to preserve the feathers, furs, and other materials used in tying fishing flies.

The first time I saw Orrin was when my fishing and fly tying buddy Ron Erlandson, brought me into the outdoor sport store to show me what and how to buy the material for tying. Orrin scared me at first with his four-day old beard and one crooked eye. It took only one visit to learn that Orrin was a gentle and kind man.

Orrin was patient, and he understood that we younger customers didn't have much money, so he'd let us buy as little as we needed. He didn't worry about standard packaging, as he gladly broke packages to accommodate our small purchases. I was a little embarrassed about my meager purchases, but Orrin would say, "That's okay, that's okay." I'd buy eight of one size hook and four of another size hook and a few of different sized corks. It seemed he made up the cost at the end because how could he figure the cost of so few hooks taken from a box of a hundred priced at 87 cents per box? I was dazzled when I gazed at the tying material in the glass cases with so many colors of chenille, silk floss, feathers, dyed deer hair, tinsels, exotic peacock and black ostrich herl.

Even though Orrin got the lion's share of the fly tiers business in town, he was a worm dunker and caught large trout. Once, when I was in his shop with Ron, Orrin took us back to show us what he had in the refrigerator. He pulled out a 21inch brown trout and a 17-inch brook trout. We, of course, asked where he caught them, and Orrin said with a twinkle in his eye, "Boys, I never reveal my secret spots." Ron said, "When I get my drivers' license, I'm going to puncture a hole in the top of a can of paint, drape the can on your car bumper, and follow the paint line to your secret spot." We all had a good laugh.

Because I loved tying flies so much and with my fly-tying bench in the basement, the only cool place during summer months, I'd tie many more flies than I needed. With so many extra flies, I decided to start selling some. Taking a piece of cardboard about 24 by 14 inches and with a razor blade, I cut halfway through the cardboard horizontally across the vertical hollow rows (just under the surface layer) of the cardboard. Then I bent the cardboard back, (where it was cut), and the vertical hollow columns under the surface were exposed. I cut about six rows, then I inserted the flies' hooks into the hollow spot in the vertical columns. The display of colorful flies looked stunning to me. I put the board of flies in a bag and toted it to school in September. The budding entrepreneur ready to do business. Sales were mighty slow. Soon I found out that kids in eighth grade didn't buy fishing flies because hardly any of them fly-fished.

One day Ron showed me how to take a safety pin and tie it into a great looking fishing fly decorative pin. In eighth grade, Sandy Coffin was my heartthrob. Finding the biggest safety pin and putting it in my fly-tying vise, I tied the most gorgeous Atlantic Salmon fly named the McGinty River Special. I used fluorescent green floss wound with oval silver tinsel for the body and yellow hackle, collared, for the throat. The tail was golden pheasant tail and the wing was black squirrel tail. At the butt end I wound green peacock herl. The neck hackle was grizzly king. For eyes I used a split steel bead painted black with a white eye and a red dot in the center. This fly was my first real work of art and a labor of love. This should put a lock on Sandy and my relationship. I gave it to her during recess one day, and she seemed impressed. When she got home from school that day, I think she shelved it because she never wore the pin, and the subject never came up. Within a couple weeks, we were no longer a couple. It would have been

124

nice to get the beautiful pin back from her because I thought I would give it to another girl someday, but I lacked the gumption to ask Sandy for it.

Spring fever is tough on an eighth-grade boy who likes baseball and fishing. In order to get excused from class because of sickness at my junior high school, we had to call home to a parent and explain that we were sick, and we were on our way home. These calls were done in front of the principal's secretary. Somehow, I mustered the nerve to fake it. I had to perform this fake call perfectly so I wouldn't be caught and called in front of our principal Vernon Peterson, mostly because Mother was a college friend of his at Eau Claire State Teachers College. I knew that mother was substitute teaching that day at Robbins Grade School, so there would be nobody home to take the call. A little nervous I held the phone receiver hard against my ear so the secretary couldn't hear the dial tone ringing on the other end. Speaking softly into the receiver I said, "Ma, it's Bill, I feel real punk, kind of like the flu, ya know, stomachache, woozy, and sore throat, so I'm coming home." For a second after hanging up the phone a twinge of fear crossed my mind as I wondered if the symptoms I described, fit with the flu. I'd never had the flu, just heard the word batted around on the playground. But by golly, the secretary didn't bat an eyelash. I'd pulled it off and was free to go.

Away I flew from school straight to Henry's Sport Shop and the familiar smell of mothballs. Orrin looked a little askance at me when I walked in the store, but he knew not to ask why I wasn't in school. He looked at my board of flies with a pleasing smile. I took my time picking and choosing my way through the display of fly-tying material. I probably bought some stuff I really didn't need because I was so happy to be there. Like a kid in a candy shop, my eyes were bigger than my coin pouch. The total bill was $2.27.

Leaving the store and ignoring the NO FOOT TRAFFIC ALLOWED sign on the railroad trestle behind the shop I scampered to the other side of the Eau Claire River. I always wondered when I used this trestle what I'd do if a train came when I was in the middle section, even though I knew the freight train tooted its whistle giving fair warning of its approach.

Along the path on the other side of the river was "Marshmallow Cave" where bums that hopped off the trains cooked food and slept. Strewn on the floor of the cave were empty cans of Sterno canned heat that some used for cooking, but more often the desperate bums drank the jellied alcohol to get drunk.

Continuing up the river to where Otter Creek emptied into it, at the Eau Claire Country Club, I stashed my fly board and notebooks in a bush, stuffed my sandwiches in my pockets, took my tennies and socks off, and waded across the creek to get to the riverbank that would get me the rest of the way up the river to the big dam. I thought I would die from the pain in my ankles from the ice-cold spring run-off water in Otter Creek. Using my handkerchief, I dried my feet, put on my socks and tennies, and continued up the river.

As I hiked up the riverbank, I felt guilty about lying to get out of school. But eventually I was able to rationalize, since every schoolboy skipped school sometime. I wasn't so unusual. I figured I was about 90% good, and that seemed good enough. The main thing is that it was spring, and I was full of fishing dreams. One thing for sure, I knew I had to get out of school that day, and there was no better place for me than on my river.

The spring breezed in the trees, and the water carried startlingly fresh scents. It seemed almost as dramatic as going into a greenhouse on a winter day. The ice melted first in the shallow riffles along the rivers' edge. It was fun watching the Greater Scaup, Bluebill, Bufflehead ducks, and especially the Hooded Mergansers with its vertical fan-shaped white crest on their heads. These minnow eaters returned early from the south. I was dazzled by the vivid mating colors of black, green, and brown on the white bodies of the handsome drakes. Robins were everywhere, and I wondered why they were fatter and less wary when they arrived from the south. It seemed that overnight the entire river and shoreline was awakened from a long winter sleep. The pussy willows were now in their fuzzy stage and that pleased me.

Finally, I found a huge limestone rock and sat down to eat my peanut butter sandwiches as I daydreamed about this summer's fishing. How the walleyes couldn't resist my black, red. and white buck tail streamers. Maybe even a northern pike this summer.

The water flowed with abandon with its wild rapids eventually smoothing out into placid deep pools. I knew how to fish this water and where the fish hung out, between the fast and slow water, along the edges of the pools and in the back eddies. This summer was going to be about catching big fish on flies I tied.

From the place where Otter Creek emptied into the Eau Claire River to the dam was approximately one mile. Within this one mile of the dam, I could hear the roar of the water tumbling over the dam as I trundled along. With my paper route money and my birthday coming up, I would be able to buy hip boots and a creel so I could wade to the really good spots. This stretch of the river had crappies, sand, walleye pike, northern pike, and bass.

Finally, it dawned on me that time was flying by, and I'd better head home before Mom got there, so I could muss up my bed to make it look used. Taking the alley to my backyard sidewalk, I slipped through the gate and was startled by, "Hello William." My heart stopped, and I stumbled as I looked in the garden. There stood Dad. He exclaimed, "And what are you doing home young man?" as he looked at my muddy tennies.

I told him I felt a little sick, but that it might not last, and I thought it best I came home to lay low. I asked him, "Are you sick too?"

He said, "Hmm, not really," and we both looked at each other with knowing looks and understood that we both had SPRING FEVER. He knew me the fisherman had to be on my river, and I knew he the gardener had to be in his garden. We both smiled as we let down our guards and agreed that it was the first really beautiful spring day. This was the first time in my life Dad let me off the hook with my misbehavior, and I felt good toward Dad-even happy, to see that he had skipped out of work early. I love this memory about Dad, how we were caught playing hooky, and how we kept it our little secret.

As I went into the house, I looked out the back porch window to see Dad with a pleasant look on his face kneeling down, picking up a clump of dirt, and crushing it in his hand as he let the dirt drain from his palm to the ground. I could tell he was redesigning his garden in his mind, and he loved it.

At the end of the summer, we moved from Eau Claire to Minneapolis. My parents continued their subscription to the Eau Claire Telegram newspaper. In 1984 mother noticed an obituary for Orrin Stanwick. In the special write up was mentioned that for several years Orrin anonymously gave a substantial sums of money to local youth fishing programs. The article quoted his nephew as saying that Orrin did this because in Orrin's words, "In all the years I had the store, I never read in the newspaper of one kid that came into my store, getting into any serious trouble."

THE 400 ARRIVES AT 5:02

A highlight in my grade school years in the 1940's was picking up Aunt Mae twice a year from the Great Northwestern 400 train at the Eau Claire depot. To me Mae represented a dashing figure traveling on a highspeed rail.

In 1939 the Chicago and Northwestern Railroad Company changed from steam to diesel and named their new train the "400." This sleek yellow beauty was advertised to be the fastest train on the American continent because it traveled between Chicago and the Twin Cities of St. Paul and Minneapolis, a distance of 400 miles, in 400 minutes. Eau Claire was the train's last stop before ending its run in the Twin Cities and its first stop leaving the Twin Cities arriving at 5:02 PM.

There was no greater thrill for me as a child than to be in the nearby town of Altoona when the "400" came roaring by on its way from Chicago to Eau Claire. Our family jumped in our 1938 Pontiac, and dad drove us to Altoona to experience the mighty "400" pass by at about 125 miles per hour. There was a yellow line painted on the landing four feet from the edge of the tracks and a sign which stated that if a child crossed the line while the train roared by, they could get sucked in under the train's wheels. Most of the other spectators stood well back from the yellow line, but dad had us stand right on the line so we would get the full impact of the glorious sight, sounds, and smells. First, we'd see the train looking like a little yellow bead nearly two miles down the tracks coming fast and someone would say, "I see it, here it comes, here it comes." Our hearts started pounding as it approached us in what seemed likes seconds. I tightened my grip on my dad's hand, holding on for dear life. This yellow thunderbolt put up an amazing crescendo of noise, dust, cinders, pebbles, and sooty smells. I'd smell the creosote that preserved the wooden railroad ties. The iron wheels pressed on steel rails, and the diesel exhaust gave off unforgettable smells unique only to the big trains. All of our senses were bombarded, and we loved it. The thrill of the passing train lasted only seconds as it rumbled by in a yellow blur. Dad would try to point out the dining car or the club car, but I was mesmerized by the wheels compressed on the rails as I thought about what it would be like being sucked under the wheels getting crushed to death. After the yellow thunderbolt passed the silence was deafening and we'd gave out a collective, "Whew, wasn't that something?"

Even after the train had passed, I kept thinking about a kid in our town we called One Arm Shea. One day One Arm Shea became impatient to get home and crawled under an idled train car at the depot. When he was under the car, another freight car hitched with it and jolted it forward over Shea's arm. Shea's arm was mangled, and he was rushed to Sacred Heart Hospital where the doctors had to amputate the arm. Was I surprised that next summer when I saw Shea at the Half Moon Lake swimming beach swimming in a straight line. I figured with only one arm he'd swim in a circle. Shea eventually went on to be the center for St. Pats High School football team.

I wondered about the people that stayed on the train seated at tables in the parlor and club cars being served by porters in white jackets and black bow ties. The dining car had an elegant look with a single flower in a tall vase on every table. To me these people who stayed on the train seemed regal as they traveled on to larger lives in the big cities of St. Paul and Minneapolis.

I tried to be the first to spot Mae getting off the train, but more often it was mother who would say, "Oh, there's Mae, there's Mae." Bursting with excitement I would try to tell her about my sports activities. Her luggage was carried from the train to a luggage area in the depot on a red and green wooden luggage wagon. I loved the wagon with its steel wheels as it went clop-a-de-clop, clop-a-de-clop, clop-a-de-clop across the brick depot platform. With suitcases secured, I'd talk a mile a minute as we jumped into the car. I could hear the man in a blue suit and hat with white trim, back on the platform yelling, "Aallll aboard! Aallll aboard!" In the back seat of the car, Mae would always give me a full package of Wrigley Spearmint Gum.

"Willy," she'd say, "Wrigley's gum is made in Chicago and sold all over the world."

I thought I was the only one getting gum, so I kept it a secret from my brothers Bob and Jon. Years later I found out that my brothers also got a package of gum when Mae saw them at the house.

Mae's arrival represented happy expectations but bringing her back to the depot always gave me an empty feeling. Aunt Mae was light and breezy and had a soft shoulder for me whenever my parents bawled me out. It made me laugh how Mae would roll her eyes when my parents reprimanded me. Her leaving also signaled a change coming because it was either the end of Christmas or summer vacation, and that meant, back to school. Mom never told me when Mae was leaving on the train because she knew it would bother me. I'd come home and there's no Mae and I'd ask, "Where's Mae?" and Mom would say, "Well Willy we just dropped her off at the train depot." On those rare occasions when I was at the depot when she left, I got a sinking feeling seeing the mighty yellow thunderbolt take her away with such dispatch, it made me feel small and insignificant. The familiar, "Aallll aboard! Aallll aboard!" Then whoosh, she would be gone down the tracks, and I would lose her for another four to five months.

My experience with the "400" ended in 1952 when we moved from Eau Claire to Minneapolis. Fortunately, eight years ago I met up with my grade school friend Norm Berg at a golf tournament in Eau Claire. Right away we started talking about childhood memories and our love for the "400". We agreed how sad it was that the "400's" run was discontinued in 1963, and ten years later the classic brownstone depot was razed. We laughed

131

when we reminisced about how our fathers took us to Altoona for the thrill of seeing the roaring train and how I held onto my father's hand tightly and how he wrapped his arms around his dad's leg.

Norm had a career as a mechanical engineer working in the railroad supply industry. Because of all his knowledge of railroading and his affinity for the "400", he decided to commission the preeminent Eau Claire railroad train artist Gil Reid to paint a watercolor of the early Chicago and Northwestern steam engine train and another painting of the new "400". Norm sent me prints of the two trains, and I love them.

I called Norm and asked, "How much can I send you for these wonderful pictures?"

Norm said, "Just make a donation to some railroad museum."

So, one day on my way to my little lake place on the Chippewa Flowage in northern Wisconsin, I stopped by the St. Croix Valley Railway Museum in Osceola, Wisconsin and wrote them a check. As I was leaving, a museum volunteer dressed in the gray and white striped hat and bib overalls came up and patted me on the back and said, "I saw that you left us a check back there, and I wanted to thank you for that, we need all the contributions we can get." We had a short chat about how we both remembered the "400."

MY RIVER

In all my life I rarely remember crossing a crick or river and not trying to get a closer look at it. Moving water fascinated me, it had a story.

In its early days, Eau Claire was often called "Mill City" or "Saw Dust City" because it had so many logging operations. It is strategically located where the Chippewa and Eau Claire rivers converge making it convenient for floating the iconic "Monarch of the North", the mighty White Pine, to the mills.

In the 1940's during grade school years Boyd Park was my first and the Eau Claire River was my second home away from home. I learned to fish moving water, and in my estimation, even as a kid I felt rivers were more educational and had greater hold on its visitors than did lakes.

My river had a dam and offered roaring rapids, pools, sluicing water over shallow rocks creating bubbling riffles, eddies, backwaters, and big calm slicks. Overall, rivers are moodier. They also have more fish species and various fly hatches all summer and some delicious aromas wafting off its gliding water.

I fished it with Dad and Bernie Behlke. Rough fish prevailed. White suckers, red horse suckers, carp, sheepshead, catfish, and dogfish. Also, it had the regular warm water game fish such as crappies, small mouth bass, and pike. The ebbs, flows, and currents make it a challenge to figure out. "A riddle to recon with", as they say. By that time I had a steel telescopic flyrod and automatic rewind reel.

Bernie Behlke and I seined minnows for bait when I bought a net six by four feet with very small mesh. With a four-foot stick fastened on each end, we could scoop up dozens of shiner and stickleback minnows. We'd put the minnows in a bucket, go to a pool next to the river, and pour the minnows in to be used later. Our holding pond. We figured it would be easier to scoop our bait from the holding pond than the wily river with its wide spaces and many nooks and crannies giving the minnows an escape route. The first time we went to our holding pond, we discovered while it was small, it was deep, and the minnows simply escaped by going underneath the net.

One day we heard about guys catching carp off the Barstow Street Bridge. So, Bernie and I thought we would fish there too. Bernie caught a big carp. We hauled it in and thought we would throw it back. All of a sudden, an old man came up to us and offered to buy the fish. Bernie and I were nonplussed. The old man said, "I'm a Jew, and with some Northern Pike I have in my refrigerator, I can make great gefilte fish." So, he bought it and walked home with it. This amazed us. We learned something that day.

As we fished along, we'd occasionally run out of worms, so we would switch to crayfish. It seemed there was a crayfish under almost every third rock. We'd use an empty can and place it behind the crayfish. With a stick, we'd nudge the critter into the can as they swam backwards. Some of the crayfish were quite large, and we only needed to be pinched once by their claws to learn a lesson.

An old-timer told me how I could catch a monster bass by using a trot-line. Of course, my biggest goal in life back then was to catch the biggest bass ever. Usually a trot-line goes from one side of the river to the other

134

side — Isaac Walton style. He suggested I simply tie the line to a willow sapling. On the hook he suggested I attach a big crayfish, and I put a sinker on the line and cast it out as far as I could. The old gent said I could leave it overnight, and in the morning I'd discover a prize fish on my line. He explained how the fish would swallow the bait deeply and the tree branch would bend when the fish tried to swim away. The flex of the branch would fight the fish like a fishing rod, tiring the fish, and the line wouldn't break because it wasn't taut. I set the system up and the next day I scampered down to the river simply beside myself with anticipation. To my delight, sure enough the branch was bouncing as my heart leapt with joy as I hauled the fish in. Dang, my surprise was a big ol' sheepshead fish, not a prestigious specie.

I hardly ever arrived or left the river without going to my favorite lookout rock. It jetted out about three feet from a ledge, seventy-five feet above the water. I loved that rock, thinking I must look majestic like a native Ojibwa perusing his happy hunting grounds. This is where I talked to myself and pondered the mysteries of life.

Being at the river gave me a sense of total freedom. There was no structure like there was at home, school, or on a baseball diamond. Often, I was there alone to visit the rock quarry and paths along the river that I was told, and of course believed, were original Ojibwa paths. I even half-heartedly considered making a raft out of trees I'd cut down and tie together. How far would I have floated? The river was a highway to discoveries on my own.

At Cub Scouts, I learned how to make a cook stove out of a big coffee can. I punched holes around the side just under the top rim. Then I filled a small can with wax from old candles and rolled up a piece of cardboard. The cardboard stuck out of the wax just enough to serve as a wick. I'd light it with a wooden farmer's match and set the can over it as it flamed, smoke coming out the holes. Baby did that stove burn, frying my bacon to perfection. So, there I sat in my little flimsy fort of tree and bush branches with my stove, hunter's knife in a sheath, and BB gun, pretending to be a hobo, pioneer, Indian scout, or hunter.

Sometimes I'd go up on the long footbridge and look down into the water to see huge fish flashing in the water as they twisted and turned chasing minnows and nymphs drifting by. Even then I thought about how lucky I was to have a river like this two blocks from my house. Seems the lessons learned were so endearing and lasted my whole life.

In the spring, that glorious time of year it seemed a fresh new world awakened. So, I'd take my first hike up the river past Otter Creek all the way to the big dam to see minnow eater diver ducks in their bright black, green and white mating colors on their way further north.

Once I ran into Billy Bunce with a handmade kayak made of long pliable wood strips covered with waterproof green canvas. He offered to sell it to me, and after some bartering, we settled on fifty cents. I loved that kayak, and with wild abandon, I paddled long stretches up and down the river putting me in water I could never reach with my fishing poles. The Huck Finn in me wondered what it would be like just floating and never stopping. Where would I end up?

Mom and Dad watched me in my kayak from the footbridge hundreds of feet above the river. Had I swamped the craft, they wouldn't have been able to get to me from way up there.

I found the perfect place between a split rock to moor my kayak. The week before school started, I went to take it out for a drift, and it was gone. Someone had floated away with my dear kayak.

Another neat experience on the river was when on 95-100 degrees evenings in late July or August, I'd notice pods of about forty fish rising, gulping flies on the surface that were so small I couldn't even see the insects. I figured these fish were crappies, so I trundled home and tied up a very tiny white fly that floated, and with my rod and reel went back the next night to see if I could catch them. Sure enough, they were surfacing again, so I made a cast and caught one. I thought I was genius to solve this riddle. I took the fish over to Ron Erlandson, and he said it was what local people call a "skip-jack". Actually, their real name is moon eyes. Ron explained that these mystery fish are rarely seen, and they seem almost ghost like. They only show themselves on those rare super hot nights.

About four or five of us kids swam in the river. The neat thing to do was to swim across the rapids to the other side — sort of a right of passage to accomplish this feat. Of course, we thought we could go straight across to the other side but found out the swift current took us down the river about twenty-five yards.

I sort of remember school starting in the middle of the week that year. That first Saturday, I returned to the river ready to join the gang for a swim and found nobody there. September was in the air, and a change in our lives began. I got such an empty feeling to lose that great fun. Our swimming was over . . . really over. My river gave a lot to me that summer and now it would rest. But how bold, generously and majestically it flowed to somewhere I couldn't imagine.

YO YOING

At least twice a summer, a man from Duncan Yo-Yo Company came to our city parks, where us kids played ball, and wowed us with his array of Duncan yo-yo's. The Duncan Yo-Yo Co. was in Luck, Wisconsin. The first time I saw this demo guy I thought he looked like some smooth, out of town jasper — sort of like a used car salesman or the kind of smoothie I'd be mesmerized by as I watched him on the midway at the county fair wowing the crowd with his kitchen cutting tools. He sure knew how to use Brylcreem on his hair, all slicked back, and he wore gabardine slacks, well pressed, sporty shoes and a very cool looking sport shirt. He seemed too perfect to by demonstrating yo-yos to us scruffy kids playing baseball at Boyd Park.

There were two models of yo-yos. The regular one priced at thirty-nine cents and the Pro at sixty cents. The Pro had a fake ruby on each side. I usually bought the thirty-nine cent one. The demo guy referred us to the dime store for our purchases.

I was obsessed with the yo-yo and learned the tricks very well. There was the loop de loop, walking the dog, motorboat, rocking the cradle, shoot for the moon, and a couple more.

A yo-yo contest was held at the base of the steps in front of City Hall. There were four of us contestants and a small crowd of onlookers. Only two of us accomplished all the tricks so they held a runoff to see who was the best. The runoff was to have us see how long we could do the loop de loop. Not how many, but who lasted longer.

I was on a roll, when I spotted my heartthrob Patsy Andrews in the crowd. So, I tried to impress her with some pizzazz in my performance, and the yo-yo went awry and I was out of the running, placing second place with no token of honor.

WESLEYAN METHODIST

Oh, how my soul soared with joy when I heard those Methodists sing their praises to the Lord on Sunday nights. I believed the Methodists were the best singers in the world. Every Sunday night, the Wesleyan Methodist Church up the alley from our house held a songfest. They would open the church windows, and the chorus would light up the whole neighborhood. I would sit on the grass across the street to hear the beautiful chorus and be inspired by their free flowing, heartfelt singing.

I wondered why they were so different from my church. I especially loved hearing the familiar songs like "Stand Up, Stand Up for Jesus" and "What a friend we have in Jesus." Even when they sang, "Jesus loves me this I Know," I was so struck by how these eighty percent adults seemed so like us Sunday school kids. Innocent, cheerful, true believers singing from the heart with a joyful bounce.

So, I asked Dad, "Why do these people sing so loud and with such joy?"

Dad just said, "Those Methodists can really sing. It's a big part of their worship, I guess."

Then I asked Reverend King, and he explained, "We feel our church is an anointed congregation, which is full of spiritualism sent from the Lord."

The singing at my Emanuel Lutheran church, the Swede church, was monotone and less bouncy. And we held no separate songfests. Even after the songfest when the people gathered outside the Wesleyan Methodist church, they seemed so spritely. They were all smiles and gave out half hugs.

I liked Reverend King, and often when I walked up the alley, I'd see him in his little garage patching his wooden rowboat. He was always patching his boat. Frequently he would tell me about some miracle product he bought at the hardware store that was guaranteed to stop leaks. Actually, I think he just liked puttering with his boat.

A minister, being an avid fisherman, impressed me. He certainly knew exactly what to use for both bass and northern pike. Reverend King and I would talk at length about when and where to use the bass plugs like the Johnson Silver Minnow (with pork rind) and the Jitterbug, as well as the Pikey (solid bodied or jointed). We talked about the famous Eppinger Daredevil spoon lure (red and white) and how it was the all-time best northern pike catcher. He insisted that one must use only the genuine Eppinger Daredevil — no cheap imitation, I agreed.

He told me about his deer hunting adventures. I figured, "Now this is a really neat preacher, one who hunts and fishes." Our discussions continued throughout the summer. I showed him the fishing flies I tied and gave him some of my best fly patterns to try.

One day Reverend King said, "Billy, how would you like to ring the bell before one of our Sunday night songfests? It's called pealing the bell, and it's important because it announces that all are welcome to sing the praises of the Lord."

My heart raced when I said, "Yes! " This was big. Ringing that gigantic bell would be such an honor. With that news, I ran home to tell my family. My mother said that it looked like the heels of my shoes were hitting my seat I was running so hard.

That Sunday I arrived at 6:45 PM to announce to the world with my clanging that the songfest started at 7:00. My friend Reverend King met me at the front door of this vine covered church and showed me to the bell. I told him how I'd sit across the street some Sundays just to hear the singing.

King said, "We Wesleyan Methodists are inspired by the songs written by Charles Wesley of England, and by the way Billy, your church sings some of his songs and of course one real popular one at Christmas, 'Hark the Herald Angels Sing' was written by Wesley."

The bell was located in a little nook next to the church entrance. I thought this whole affair was so holy. I peeked in the church sanctuary, and it looked so sacred and serious with the lofty pulpit looming over the pews. What a privilege to have this big responsibility!

Rev. King said, "Pull down the rope then let it swing. You'll get the rhythm. You'll see. Don't let go of the rope or you will lose control."

I looked up at that huge bell. The rope was old and thick and had a big knot at the end where I gripped it. Reverend King said, "OK, you can start." My heart was pounding. I pulled down, and the bell clanged so loud I couldn't believe it. Holding tight on the upswing, the rope lifted me off the floor about six inches. I was startled and a little frightened. I landed on my feet and just kind of stopped. King said, "Come on keep going. The process is pull and let the rope lift you, and when you land pull again." Doing just that, I got the bell ringing like crazy.

I was proud as I thought surely Jesus or God knew exactly who I was, where I was, and what a good deed I was performing. Maybe even Wesley was looking over my shoulder. This was the most religious thing I had ever done. There I was really letting it rip. Up and down I bounced, the sound was deafening, but thrilling. It was hard to believe I was the bell ringer for Wesleyan Methodist Church! To me it even seemed like there were more people showing up that night. After I finished, I just floated home.

The minister said I could do it again sometime. The next week Rev. King was on vacation, and in two weeks, our family moved to Minneapolis. Things seemed to move so fast. My parents deferred telling me about the move until the last minute. I never even had a chance to say goodbye to my friend, the sporty preacher, but I'll always have that sweet memory of being the bell ringer that rousted the joyful singers.